A "Digging Deeper" Study Guide
Book "C"

D1469872

World Empires, World Missions, World Wars

Napoleon through the Korean War

by Diana Waring

Graphics and design by Isaac Waring

"How lovely on the mountains are the feet of him who brings good news, who proclaims peace, who brings glad tidings of good things, who proclaims salvation..." Isaiah 52:7

Special Thanks to all those who helped make this project happen:

- all the librarians at Grace Balloch Memorial Library, especially Kathy Follette without whose gracious and invaluable help I could never have located the bazillions of books included in this study guide;

- my message board friends who pray for me;

- all the families who used **Ancient Civilizations and the Bible** and **Romans, Reformers, Revolutionaries** and were kind enough to tell us they loved it;

- and my children:
  Isaac (our company's illustrator par excellence),
      Michael (the war expert among us)
          Melody (the cheerful one who keeps us going).

As always, this project was the result of team-work. It would never have happened without my wise, patient, and generous husband, Bill. In fact, he contributed most of the musical know-how and several excellent project ideas. What a blessing!

Table of Contents

WHAT YOU NEED TO HAVE:

1. **"What in the World's Going On Here?" tapes, Volume Two -**
   These tapes will give you the historical framework and the "big picture" to be able to understand each time period. They are fun to listen to, energetic, and enthusiastic, so please, no whining!

2. **"True Tales From the Times of World Empires, World Missions, World Wars" audio tape -**
   Ninety minutes of more stories from this time period, including the Cold War, the Korean War, and Jim Elliot.

3. **A Bible -**
   There are Bible passages listed at the beginning of each chapter which will help you evaluate the history you are studying through the lens of God's Word.

4. **A good reference book -**
   You may use a history textbook or encyclopedia for a reference, but my recommended choice is the Kingfisher Illustrated History of the World. It is available through many homeschool providers and through any general bookstore.

5. **Map/Timeline Pack - WWW -**
   This provides the twelve boundary outline maps including Europe, the Middle East, Africa, and the world, as well as a fill-in timeline to place on the wall or a door. If you prefer, your students may create their own maps and timeline.

6. **A library card -**
   It is the best "investment" you will make.

SUGGESTED RESOURCES:

1. **"From Jerusalem to Irian Jaya - A Biographical History of Christian Missions"**
   by Ruth A. Tucker
   This is the best book available on the history of world missions. Included are short biographies of missionaries all over the world, categorized by their geographical area of service. I consider this an indispensable resource for the study of **World Empires, World Missions, World Wars**.

2. **"More Than Conquerors - Portraits of Believers from All Walks of Life"**
   Edited by John Woodbridge
   This is THE book of biographies of Christians from the 1800's and 1900's! The categories are: Politics & Public Life, Missions, Writers, Evangelists, Preachers, Sports & Entertainment, Reformers, Student Work, Thinkers, and Industry & Commerce. Written by dozens of contributors, this book will truly give you an encouraging insight into men and women who served the Lord. I would strongly suggest you purchase this book for your resource library.

3. **"The Gift of Music - Great Composers and Their Influence"**
   by Jane Stuart Smith & Betty Carlson
   This is an excellent resource book for the music section of **World Empires, World Missions, World Wars**. Learn about the most important composers from the 1600's through the 1900's. What we really appreciated about this book was that it was not merely a collection of biographies. Rather, the authors provided the lens by which we can see the worldvew of each of these composers. Another must-have.

4. **"The 100 Most Important Dates in Church History"** (formerly titled **Dates with Destiny**)
   by A. Kenneth Curtis, J. Stephen Lang, and Randy Petersen
   Beginning with the year 64 in Rome and continuing to 1976, this book is filled with short descriptions of events and people within the Church.

WHAT YOU NEED TO DO:

1. **Obtain the items from the "What You Need To Have" list above.**

2. **Go to the library and get your books ordered.**
   You will find dozens of books to choose from in this study guide, and there will be many more possibilities for related titles in the library.

3. **Make a plan.**
   There are lots of possibilities for activities in this study guide. With your students, choose which activities will be done. This planning time should take about two hours per month.

4. **Read, read, read.**
Have your students read throughout the study of each unit. The more books, the merrier!

5. **Talk, talk, talk.**
Engage your students in the Talk Together questions listed, or the questions that come up during the study.
To have you paying attention to their questions will whet their appetite for a lifetime of learning!

6. **Think, think, think.**
The next phase will stretch your brain cells. With your students, choose topics from the Research and Reporting items.

7. **Hands-on stuff.**
Are your students hands-on learners? Then this is where the fun begins! Feel free to intersperse some of these activities among the first and second phase activites.

8. **Go creative!**
The fourth phase of every unit is where the creative juices can really flow. Your students will be able to choose from suggestions for writing, cartooning, drama, or rhyming.

9. **Final exam...**
There are NO exams. This is real, interest-based, exciting learning! You will find many opportunities for evaluation as you interact with your students.

For a more detailed explanation, please turn to How To Use This Study Guide, page vi.

FREQUENTLY ASKED QUESTIONS:

Q. **How long do we need to spend each day?**
A. It depends upon how old your children are! High school students could easily spend several hours each day pursuing all the different subject areas. Elementary students might only need to spend an hour or two per day. Each family has unique students and unique needs, so tailor this to your own situation.

Q. **Can I find all of these books in my library?**
A. Not quite. There are some books listed that have been written and published by Christian authors, and might not be available through your library. Check the library first, then check with your homeschool vendor and/or Christian book store. However, the vast majority of books are available through the library or through interlibrary loan.

Q. **Do I need all of the books listed?**
A. No. I have listed all of the books I was able to find that were appropriate so that you would have the best possible chance of finding SOME of the books. If you cannot find a particular suggested title, ask your librarian to help you find a similar book.

Q. **Do we have to answer every question?**
A. No. There are many suggested questions for each unit so that your family will be able to find a FEW questions that are interesting and understandable at their level. You will need to have your students begin reading the library books or looking in your resource books before they will be able to answer most of the questions. However, feel free to answer as many as you like! Use the Unit Objectives to guide your choices.

Q. **Do we have to do every research project?**
A. No. There are many research projects listed in order to appeal to the students' different interests and different levels. The "Brain Stretchers" are to challenge the more advanced students. My suggestion is to do between one and three research projects for each unit. Again, use the Unit Objectives to guide your choices.

Q. **Do we have to do all of the activities in the Hands-On section?**
A. Not always. These activities respond to the learning style demand of certain students, and will cultivate a desire to learn. If you choose to skip an activity in one chapter, please be sure to pick it up in the next. I would like to suggest that you do not skip the art appreciation or architecture sections as they will provide an excellent visual tool for understanding the changes in history.

Q. **Where do we find the art and architecture photos?**
A. Check your encyclopedias under "Paintings," "Architecture," or the name of the specific artist. Then check the library for art history books, including the specific time periods such as "modern art." If you are on-line, check the search engines for the specific paintings, buildings, or artists. Finally, any artist, art teacher, or architect could be contacted for their resources and input.

Q. **How will I know if I have covered every thing?**

A. The Unit Objectives listed at the beginning of each chapter will be your guide in determining if you have covered the essentials. If your students can demonstrate what they have learned concerning that objective, you have accomplished that goal. However, there are many other wonderful "rabbit trails" they may wish to pursue during each historic time period. Have fun!

Q. **There are no answers in the back of the book! What do I do?**

A. Relax. One of the most powerful principles of education is the value of "discovery"! This means that if the student really wants to know the "why," the "what," the "when," or the "how," they will be motivated to search out the answer. When they DISCOVER it for themselves, then it is learned long term. This is quite different from, "Read the chapter and answer the questions at the back of the book." That is the "canned approach" to learning, and it is not generally retained, nor is it interesting. My suggestion to you is to relax, get your rest at night, and let your students do the work of discovering the answers in the resource and library books. If they are younger, you can help them with the discovery process. Whatever you do, let it be a treasure hunt!

Q. **Can my high schooler do this?**

A. Yes! **World Empires, World Missions, World Wars** was designed to be used by the whole family, and high school students will find exciting challenges and interesting moments in history adequate to the requirements for high school credit as they read, research, and create. My high school students have really enjoyed the humorous approach as well as the delight of having history open up to them.

Q. **Can my young student do this?**

A. Yes! There are some books that can be read out loud, art projects they can accomplish, cooking projects to help make and taste, music to sing, drama skits to perform, and, of course, discussions 'round the dinner table!

Q. **Are there different levels of books, questions, and projects?**

A. Yes. Help your students choose the items that are most appropriate to their level.

Q. **Does this cover every subject?**

A. No. Depending on the age of your students, you may need to add phonics, math, science, spelling, and grammar. For high school students, we suggest finding an English Literature textbook to given appropriate introductory information and guide notes about some of the literature you will be reading during this course.

Q. **What do we need for this course?**

A. Check the "What You Need to Have to Use This Guide" page.

Q. **We can't find the answers to some of the questions. What do we do?**

A. In the "Talk Together" questions, there may be some open-ended questions that have no final answer. It is important to help your students learn the difference between areas we can know certainly and areas we can only speculate about. It is also highly appropriate to say, "I don't know the answer to this. Let's see if we can find someone who does!" Then check with your library, other home-schoolers, online, etc. If all else fails, ask me!

HOW TO USE THIS STUDY GUIDE:

1. **Order your books for each unit from the library prior to starting the chapter.**

2. **Plan to spend approximately one week for each learning phase.**
   Read more about Learning Styles in the next few pages.
   "Meet the People" ....The "Feeler" learning style   "Teaching Time" .... The "Thinker" learning style
   "Hands-On" ....The "Sensor" learning style   "Idea Time" .... The "Intuitor" learning style

3. **Plan to spend approximately one month per chapter.**
   Nine chapters = Nine months. Some chapters might take more time, some less.

4. **Listen to the appropriate "What in the World's Going On Here?" tape.**
   The tapes will provide a foundational framework on which your students will build their deeper understanding of history. An outline of the specific portion of the taped message you will use is included in each chapter.

5. **Read the books - Biographies, Historical Fiction, Non-Fiction, and Classic Literature.**
   There are lots of wonderful books to read during this year! Gather up as many as you can find from your shelves, the library, homeschool vendors, the used book stores, etc. You may want to designate a special bookshelf just for the books used in this study, and encourage the students to "graze" to their hearts' delight! It will be helpful to the students if they are reading in the various resources throughout the duration of the entire chapter's activities.

In this study we will discover the literature of the great writers, and have the opportunity to read the great masterpieces of world history, such as Charles Dickens' **Oliver Twist**, Jane Austen's **Pride and Prejudice**, Rudyard Kipling's **Kim**, L.M. Montgomery's **Anne of Green Gables**, J.R.R. Tolkien's **The Lord of the Rings**, and many more.

We will also spend time reading literature about these historic times. Biographies and historic fiction are excellent ways to introduce students to different time periods, and there are dozens to choose from in this study guide. The student will have ample opportunity to read wonderful literature - which will expand their understanding of history!

An important point to remember: Read material from various sources!
If there are ten biographies of Napoleon, be sure to read at least two or three. Different authors focus on different aspects of a person's life, and if you read more than one author, it will help to give your students a more balanced and a fuller understanding of the people in history.

6. **Discuss together the questions you have selected.**
   You can do this in the car, around the dining table, snuggled up on the couch, walking in the park... The important thing is to really give yourself over to these discussion times, engage your students fully as you consider issues together. Your children will benefit from your musings and ponderings, and you will be astounded to hear the kinds of things they will come up with. Remember, discussion time is not the Spanish Inquisition! (- though you may end up talking about the Inquisition.) It is a good time to listen to each other. Remind each one to show courtesy to the others. And remember, there is no such thing as a "dumb" question. Watch for answers to these questions as they are discovered in subsequent readings.

7. **Do the Timeline.**
   Creating your own visual timeline will really make a difference in making the connections between people, places and events in history. Directions given in each chapter will help direct this activity.

8. **Do research and report projects on the topics you have selected.**
   This is the "roll up your sleeves and go to work" section of the chapter. Your students will find answers in resource books, encyclopedias, biographies, non-fiction, historical fiction, and online. Allow each of your students who is old enough to participate in this portion to choose their own project(s) as it is far more educational and satisfying when one is truly interested in the research topic. Reports can be long or short, formal or informal, technically illustrated or plain - depending on the age and interests of your students. (One suggestion: If your student can not find adequate answers on a research question, and you are not able to help them find answers, allow them to choose another question.)

9. **Have fun with Vocabulary.**
   The vocabulary words are included as a help to you and your students, to make sure that they are familiar with the terms in each chapter.

10. **Find out where all these people, places, and events are located using the Maps and Mapping section.**
    It may take a little digging to find the answers, but the rewards will be worth it! Your students will be able to see for themselves the difficulties overcome in traveling the oceans, the deserts, the mountains, etc. They will see how incredible the conquests of Napoleon were when they see how much territory was involved; they will appreciate the vastness of the British colonial structure when they see that the sun truly "never set on the British Empire;" they will discover how amazing the China Inland Mission's penetration into China really was; and much, much more.

11. **Discover how art history/art appreciation suggestions make history come alive!**
    Take the time to discover more about the art described in each chapter. It will provide a priceless visual window into history! Find the paintings in encyclopedias, art history books, and online. You may wish to investigate David Quine's **Adventures in Art**, which provides an incredible "look" into art history and how it relates to human thought.

12. **Do the art projects which are related to that period of history.**
    There's nothing like getting your hands dirty to help you learn more! As much as possible, try some of the projects listed. Your students will grow in their appreciation of what the great artists faced and accomplished as they try their own hand at creating art.

13. **Study the architecture of the time.**
    I was amazed to see how well the architecture of a time reflects the history of that time. The Neo-Classic monuments, the Gothic Revival buildings, the Art Deco structures and others, hold many lessons about their moments of creation.

14. **Learn about science in history.**
    During this time period in history (from Napoleon to the Korean War), there were astounding discoveries in the area of science. Discover with your students the way science fits into history, and enjoy the projects!

15. **Listen to the music of the masters.**
    From Beethoven to Stravinsky, from Tchaikovsky to Poulenc, we will be studying the great composers and the different eras in music from the 1800's to the 1900's.

16. **Cook foods related to the chapter.**
    Cooking involves at least three of the senses - smell, taste, sight - so it is a wonderful tool to help make the history of a time come alive! Use my suggested recipes as a jumping off place into other foods and other cultures.

17. **Write creative stories, limericks, poems, and journalistic masterpieces.**
    You will probably notice a lot of humor in the suggested stories and poems. Humor appeals to students in the area of creative writing. Allow your students to choose their own topics for writing, if they prefer.

18. **Try your hand at political cartooning.**
    Some folks have it, some folks don't, and some folks have never tried! It is a very creative exercise to create a political cartoon because it involves not only artistic skill but a firm grasp of the subject matter as well.

19. **Put on a play, skit, or puppet show.**
    Let the whole family be involved in these dramatic presentations. Even the youngest can be a part, and it is such fun to have the family work together in this way. It is also a marvelous place for the "hams" in your family to have a chance to express themselves.

20. **Create a final presentation to share with family and friends.**
    You will probably not want to do this for every chapter, but I would like to encourage you to allow the time and trouble to do this at least once! It is amazing to see how much more our students will be motivated to study and to learn and to prepare when they know that they will have an audience to listen to them. And remember the old saying - "The best way to learn something is to teach it!"

The *Spinning Plates Effect* of History:

You will soon notice in this study guide that there is a lot going on in history! There are crowned monarchs, scientific discoveries, artistic geniuses, massive monuments, world wars, influential philosophers, mighty missionaries, colonizing countries and more. You might begin to feel like this man who is keeping all his plates spinning:

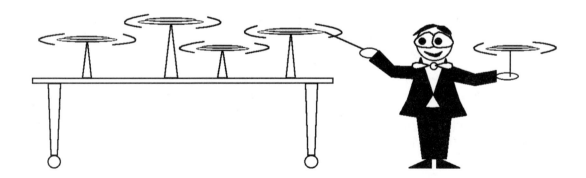

My advice is to sample a bit of everything, and when you discover something you and your students find intriguing - take your time and enjoy it. In other words, **DIG IN!**

Worldviews in the Study of History:
Our Approach to History

When Bill and I were attending a secular university, I took some anthropology courses. Anthropology is the scientific study of mankind, especially its origins, development, customs, and beliefs. At the very introduction to General Anthropology, I was alarmed and put on guard because it was announced that Christian missionaries were **always destructive** to the cultures they went to convert; that by changing the primitive peoples' belief systems and destroying their uniqueness with a western religion, the missionaries had ruined them. In sharp contrast, the anthropologists were engaged in the "scientific" study of these people groups and wouldn't think of changing anything about them (much like a "nature" photographer will take pictures of predators killing a baby elephant without doing anything to help preserve the life of the baby.)

One particular people group that we studied extensively in this class made a deep and lasting impression on me. They were the Dani of Irian Jaya (Papau New Guinea shares the same South Pacific island). The anthropologists studying the Dani had filmed them during the time that a small argument between a few escalated into a violent battle with many men killed. Throughout the film and the documents prepared on the Dani, we were "treated" to a look at a Stone Age tribe that was brutal, violent, aggressive, and dominated by a religion of evil spirits. This "scientific study" of the Dani left me with the sense of darkness and hopelessness because of the despair and depravity in this people group.

Twenty years later, we picked up the book, **Torches of Joy**, by John Dekker (YWAM Publishing). Can you imagine the astonishment and delight when I discovered that this book was about a Christian missionary family that devoted themselves to the Dani people?! It described a complete, miraculous turnaround for these precious "Stone Age" people. The Dani burned their fetishes, forsook tribal warfare, and began to walk in the joy and freedom of their deliverer, Jesus Christ. The missionaries taught them basic medical knowledge, hygiene, nutrition; built fish ponds and imported fish so the Dani could increase the protein in their meager diets; helped set up trade stores which the Dani owned and operated; taught them how to read, so they could read the Bible in the newly written form of their oral language; discipled them in Biblical principles so the Dani men began to truly love their wives (rather than treating them as slaves), as well as loving their neighbors as themselves; appointed native leadership for the young church, which resulted in Dani missionaries actually going out to other tribal peoples in Irian Jaya!

The difference between these two approaches, between the "scientific study" of a Stone Age tribe by the anthropologists and the compassionate, life-giving ministry of the Christian missionaries, is the difference between darkness and light; the difference between secular humanism and biblical Christianity; it reveals how godless man looks at cultures and how God looks at people. Seeing with God's heart will prevent bigotry and hate, replacing it with outreach and compassion.

As we study world history together, please remember this illustration because it will be the difference between:

- learning merely the facts and figures of a people group,

OR

- seeing fully the loving heart of God towards those people.

The first will give head knowledge of important data that may impress our audience and make us think that we really know a lot. However, the second will give heart understanding of God's involvement in human history, so that we might be effective ministers in obedience to the Lord of all.

As we learn the details of world history, of kingdoms and empires, scientific discoveries, explorations, philosophy, art, music, architecture and more, we will begin to see God's fingerprint on the lives of people and cultures. History will become a window of adventure as we observe His faithfulness and provision for those who seek Him, His timing in raising up one nation and bringing down another, His perfect ability to work through imperfect people, and His wonderful plan to bring us to Himself, which is revealed in the Bible.

So Many Books, So Little Time!

Unless we have the opportunity to:
- actually travel the world;   - visit all the museums;
- see all the paintings;   - visit all the architectural wonders;
- interview monarchs, popes, artists, composers, peasants, explorers, and scientists;
we will not really comprehend history.
That is, UNLESS we read books!!

Books will unlock the doors to learning:
- *Meet William Carey, the shoemaker whose scholarly translations of Indian languages gained him honor throughout India;*
- *Witness the decisive meeting between Commodore Perry and the Japanese who had refused to allow foreigners on their shores for 200 years;*
- *Relive the famous meeting between David Livingstone and Henry Stanley in the depths of the African jungle;*
- *Discover the amazing mission of Amy Carmichael to save the temple prostitutes in training - little girls - in India;*
- *Witness the repercussions of the Victorian family feud between King George and Kaiser Wilhelm II which brought the world to war;*
- *Observe T.E. Lawrence, "Lawrence of Arabia," outsmart the Germans and the Turks with his army of Arabs;*
- *See the miraculous deliverance in WWII when 338,000 Allied soldiers were rescued off the beaches of Dunkirk.*

Where do we learn all of these wonderful, fascinating, intriguing stories? In books, books, and more books! There are books about art, architecture, wars, city planning, construction techniques, costumes, music, science, and more. There are picture books, children's books, fictional books, boring books, fascinating books, books to be shared and books to be discarded.

Does this mean we need to take out a second mortgage to purchase all of these books?! NO! It means we need to become well acquainted with our library, our librarians, the interlibrary loan system, the university libraries, the state libraries, school libraries, church libraries, and your friends' and neighbors' libraries.

The library system is a wonderful resource - let's learn how to use it!

Using your local library:

- search card catalog or computer by author, title, or subject;
- go on safari - hunt out the best books in the library;
- photocopy the book list from each chapter of **World Empires, World Missions, World Wars** and have your librarian help you search for titles on interlibrary loan.

Dewey Decimal System

Divided into 10 major categories:

000 - 099 General works (reference)
100 - 199 Philosophy
200 - 299 Religion
300 - 399 Social sciences (folklore, legends, government, manners & customs)
400 - 499 Language (dictionaries, grammars)
500 - 599 Pure Science (math, astronomy, chemistry, nature study)
600 - 699 Technology (applied sciences - aviation, building, homemaking)
700 - 799 Arts (photography, drawing, painting, music, sports)
800 - 899 Literature (plays, poetry)
900 - 999 History (ancient and modern, geography, travel)

Fiction books are alphabetized by author; separate categories for westerns, mysteries, paperbacks, Christian fiction. Same categories and separation for Children's Books - Juvenile. (Easy or Beginner Books are listed according to author's last name.)

Also, look in these valuable places for more information:

- Reader's Guide to Periodic Literature (especially **National Geographic** and **Christian History** for their invaluable articles on historic people and issues);
- Vertical Files;
- Audio books, educational videos, music, and more;
- Interlibrary Loan.

Four excellent and interesting series appropriate for students in this study are:
World Landmark Books (mid-elementary and up)
Horizon Caravel Books (upper elementary and up)
Cambridge Introduction to History (upper elementary and up)
World Leaders Past and Present (Junior High and up)

Other places to find books:

- purchase new from stores, conventions, mail order catalogs, book clubs, etc.;
- purchased used from used book stores, garage sales, library & school book sales, other homeschoolers, etc.;
- put them on your Christmas list, birthday list, etc.;
- barter;
- co-op a homeschool library resource center through your support group.

Family Style Studies

We have always found that studying history together as a family makes it fascinating! Since we all have such different interests, studying as a family allows many more topic discussions to come up, many more rabbit trails to be followed, and many varying opinions about "why this happened" to be expressed. There is a "synergy" - (synergy: the whole is greater than the sum of the parts) - that occurs when the whole family researches different aspects of a civilization and then shares their insights with each other!

NOTE: Preschoolers are obviously not up to the "research" mode yet, but they can certainly be involved with skits, building forts, sculpting play dough, tasting the "authentic" recipes, etc., as a connection with the unit.

Here are some suggestions about how to make history a "family time!"

- *Keep a common thread running in the family. One of the best ways we have found is to read aloud the most interesting book that will appeal to everyone.*

- *Ask open ended questions and assignments so each can answer in their own way: "Of all the things we've learned about this culture, what aspect has been most interesting (i.e. art, writing, weaponry, etc.) to you? OK, do a project on that!" or "Research the everyday life in this historic time of a farmer, a soldier, a mother, a daughter, a ruler - whatever you would have wanted to be. Then tell us about it."*

- *Get lots of books from the library and from other resources that deal with a variety of topics pertinent to the time period. Do not assign which books the children must read, rather allow them to choose what look's interesting to them - and then let them tell the others what they learned from that book.*

- *Provide lots of opportunities to share with each other about what is being learned. This is not a "test," but an "I can't wait to tell you about this!" atmosphere. Dinner time, car rides across town, last half hour before bed, walks to the park are all great times for sharing the fascinating "stuff" you're learning.*

- *Have fun with the art projects, the science projects, the drama skits, and all of the other areas which the whole family can do together.*

Record Keeping & Evaluations

There are many different ways to track your student's work and progress. High school students will need a more thorough record kept than elementary students, and different teachers prefer different methods of keeping track of what's been accomplished. For a thorough description of record keeping, please check your state's requirements (available through homeschool support groups), and refer to such resources as Gayle Graham's **How to Homeschool**, Diana McAllister's **Homeschooling the Highschooler**, Diana Waring's **Beyond Survival: A Guide to Abundant Life Homeschooling**, and other books.

Some possibilities for tracking the work are:

- Keep a simple log of books read, projects done, topics covered (can be done by student or teacher)
- Make a portfolio of major projects completed
- Record the hours spent, subject studied
- Plan objectives with student, determine whether objectives were met (contract agreement)
- There are nine units in this study and records can be kept accordingly:
  - each unit can be recorded separately (i.e. Napoleon & Early Missions)
  - the entire study guide can be treated as one course (**World Empires, World Missions, World Wars**)

Some possibilities for evaluating the work are:

- **Narration** - allow your students to tell in their own words what has been read (a wonderful way to discover whether they fully understand the important points of a book).
- **Discussion** - ask open-ended questions to permit a free flowing conversation about what is being learned.
- **Presentation** - give opportunity for your students to share what they have learned in a more formal setting.
- **Written reports** - fictional stories, poetry, dramas, essay questions, research reports, and more are all possible means of determining your student's mastery of the subject.

Bloom's Taxonomy

For those who are interested, Bloom's Taxonomy is a tool to help teachers establish their educational objectives. Highly regarded and widely used among educators, it is used to assure that a course of study challenges the thought processes of each student from the youngest to the most developed.

In our study guide, we have followed the wisdom of using Bloom's Taxonomy in the development of our lesson suggestions. (**Important Note:** You DON'T need to understand Bloom's Taxonomy in order to benefit from the use of it in this study guide!)

Incorporated throughout **World Empires, World Missions, World Wars** are questions, activities, and assignments that cover the range of the six categories described in **Bloom's Taxonomy**:

- Knowledge: ....Remembering, drilling, listing, repeating
- Comprehension: ....Understanding, identifying, reviewing, explaining, reporting
- Application: ....Solving, using, interpreting, demonstrating, illustrating
- Analysis: ....Analyzing, experimenting, debating, comparing, questioning
- Synthesis: ....Creating, formulating, designing, arranging
- Evaluation: ....Judging, evaluating, appraising, establishing criteria

Learning Styles

This study guide has been designed to incorporate the four learning styles into each unit. For the parent/teacher this is not a constant cause for decision making and possibly confusing choices, but an assurance of thoroughness on the author's part - there will be material to attract each of your students and to provide a multi-faceted approach to understanding history.

A brief explanation of these four learning styles follows (for more information, please read Diana Waring's **Beyond Survival: A Guide to Abundant Life Homeschooling**, Cynthia Tobias' book **The Way They Learn**, or Alta Vista's **Learning Styles and Tools**). What follows is a sketch of each of the learning styles. Perhaps you will recognize your students among these descriptions.

The Feeler

This is the "people person" learning style. A Feeler wants to know the people perspective, i.e. how this subject affects people, how does this impact our lives now, who were the people of history as opposed to the events or the things? This learner needs to be in good relationship with the people around him - his teacher, siblings, friends, etc. They love to be with other people in one-on-one conversations and in group activities, especially when they are part of a "team effort".

The Thinker

"Give me the facts, ma'am, just the facts." The Thinker has a black and white approach to knowledge, wanting authoritative input, not just someone's opinions. This learner truly enjoys using textbooks, encyclopedias, charts, diagrams. There is a need to know exactly what is expected, when it is expected, what, exactly, are the requirements of an assignment, project, etc. They are organized and expect organization.

The Sensor

The "hands-on," get-it-done-now person! The Sensor is the one who can make projects happen - taking them beyond the "blueprint" stage and into production. This learner does NOT enjoy sitting for long periods of time, looking through books for information (which is the Thinker's cup of tea!), or cuddling up on the couch to discuss things for hours on end (which appeals to the Feeler!). Instead, the Sensor prefers to be involved with things that can be efficiently accomplished, and that require more physical than mental work.

The Intuitor

"Wait! I have an idea!" The Intuitor is the one brimming over with ideas about how this might have happened, or about how your family might put on a play for the whole city portraying an historic event, or about what it must have been like to live in ancient times, and on and on. This learner is very good at coming up with suggestions, but is much less interested in seeing things through to completion. The Intuitor needs a lot of flexibility in schedule, and a "safe haven" for suggesting and trying out ideas. (It's not helpful to squash ALL of their ideas, no matter how bizarre!!!)

Learning Modalities

There is often confusion about the differences between the four learning styles and the terms visual, auditory and kinesthetic. To clarify what is meant by learning modalities, i.e. visual, auditory, kinesthetic, consider this analogy. A friend from the other side of the country wants to come to your house for a visit. They may choose to fly, to take the train, or to come by bus - whichever they prefer. In the same way, each of us has a preferred method of transporting information to our brains. Some grasp new material best by reading it (visual), others by hearing someone talk (auditory), still others by manipulating it (kinesthetic).

Any of these modalities can be found in each of the four learning styles. For instance, your son may be a Thinker who receives information best by hearing it, while your daughter may be a Thinker who must read the instructions in order to remember them. You may be a Sensor who needs to simply pull all the nuts and bolts out of the bag to assemble the kit (forget reading the instructions!) Perhaps your spouse is an Intuitor who can figure out how to create a new brick design after simply seeing samples in a book, while your Intuitor neighbor could hear a description of a new recipe for cherry pie and then springboard off into a new recipe for cherry coffeecake.

Please remember, these are not labels intended to put a person into a "box." Rather, they are tools that help us understand and appreciate one another. Particularly, if you find that a student is not grasping the material, or is in conflict with you about an assignment, be sure to consider these learning styles and learning modalities to see if perhaps you could use a different approach in your presentation.

Cycle Approach Used in Each Unit

With these four learning styles in mind, the cycle approach used in this study guide will begin with a phase to introduce the people involved, which the Feeler will love. Then we will proceed to the "hard facts" phase, which excites the Thinker. The next phase will be right up the Sensor's alley with lots of hands-on projects, followed by the open-ended "possibilities" phase which will make the Intuitor soar. All students, regardless of their learning style, will benefit from this four-phase cycle approach because it reinforces the new material over and over again. Also, because each of us have a combination of learning styles, learning modalities, as well as giftings, talents and interests, the cycle approach will provide a well-rounded blend of study activities for each of your unique students.

Phase #1: Grab 'Em!
(the Feeler)

History:
- **What in the World's Going on Here?, Volume 2** tapes
- The names of the people, places, events
- Preview presentation - video, audio, read aloud, explain
- "If you were there" - intro to the impact of the location and terrain on people and cultures
- Discussing the impact of a ruler on conquered people
- Learning about family issues

Language Arts:
- Reading biographies, historical fiction
- Answer the questions "who-how?" in written or verbal form
- Snapshot bio (most important aspects of a person's life) written in the history journal or in a separate notebook
- Journal - regular entry to track what is being learned

Phase #2: Teach 'Em!
(the Thinker)

History:
- Identify and follow strands - warfare, technology, apparel, architecture, people groups, agriculture, transportation, etc.
- Seminar outline from **What in the World's Going on Here?**
- Build a timeline
- Vocabulary list
- Reasearch and report
- Compile additional information for personalized unit studies
- "When?" in relation to other events, other civilizations
- Charting out each empire's key leaders, cities, wars, etc.

Language Arts:
- Reading factual accounts of history
- Written or verbal or video report
- Answer the "why?" "what?" "how?"
- Researching in library - periodicals, non-fiction history section
- Summarizing, compiling

Computer:
- On-line - check out information available on the Internet (Caution: parental supervision)
- CD-ROM's/DVD's about history

Phase #3: Apply 'Em!
(the Sensor)

Geography:
- Maps to fill in
- Topographical maps - to study
- Learn climate and terrain

Arts and Crafts:
- Models
- Collage
- Costuming
- Making props for productions
- Papier Maché - puppet heads, masks, mosaics, buidings
- Painting
- Observation - paintings, sculptures, artwork
- Cooking
- Video productions - computer art
- Drawing, coloring

Architecture:
- Looking at architectural styles of the 1800's - 1900's

Music:
- Listening to the great composers

Science:
- Experimentation and discovery

Phase #4: Release 'Em!
(the Intuitor)

Creative Writing:
- Short story
- Journalism - interview characters from history
- Illustrate a children's book
- Poetry
- Rhymes

Art:
- Cartoons
- Illustrations

Drama:
- Role-playing
- Puppet shows
- Plays

Extrapolate:
- "How did ...?" or "What if ...?" questions
- Plan a presentation using drama, music, art, puppetry which explains what has been learned in the unit
- Teach the younger students some aspect of living in history using a creative approach to capture their attention

Unit One

Napoleon & Early Missions

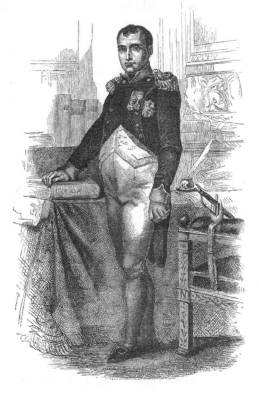

Napoleon Bonaparte

Unit Objectives:

- To learn about the life of Napoleon and his influence on the world;

- to discover Lord Nelson's importance for England and his impact on the world;

- to study Haiti's successful slave revolt under Toussaint L'Ouverture, and the impact of Wilberforce's movement to abolish slavery in England;

- to see the early beginnings of the modern missions movement, and meet some of the great missionary pioneers such as Carey and Judson;

- to understand the difference between an "absolute monarchy" and a "constitutional monarchy."

Meet the People & Study the Countries:

Here are some people you might meet in this unit:

In the Church:

William Carey   Adoniram Judson   William Wilberforce
Clapham Community   Robert Haldane   Hans Nielsen Hague

In the World:

Napoleon   Lord Nelson   Toussaint L'Ouverture
Czar Alexander   Duke of Wellington   King George III
Francis of Austria   Ludwig van Beethoven   Franz Joseph Haydn

You might wish to study one of these places in depth during this unit:

France   Haiti   Burma
Spain   Louisiana

- **The Holy Bible**
  Matthew 28:18-20; Mark 13:7-8

- **Napoleon** by Manfred Weidhorn
  Of all the biographies on Napoleon for children, this was my absolute favorite. The author's goal is to show how astonishing was Napoleon's life. Very readable, very interesting. Highly recommended!   **Upper elem & up**

- **Napoleon and the Battle of Waterloo** - A World Landmark Book, by Frances Winwar
  Written for younger children, this is a sympathetic look at one of the greatest conquerors of all time.   **Elementary & up**

- **Napoleon** - Longman Great Lives Series, by Anthony Masters
  This book has lots of illustrations, paintings and a chronology of events in Napoleon's life. It is an excellent introduction to this powerful man, showing how absolute power corrupts absolutely.   **Upper elem & up**

- **Napoleon Bonaparte** by Brian Williams
  A very brief biography for children, this book is filled with color drawings of Napoleon and his times. A good "primer."   **Elementary & up**

- **The True Story of Napoleon - Emperor of France** by Anthony Corley
  This was among the most interesting, most readable biographies on Napoleon for children. Mr. Corley's anecdotes about Napoleon bring the story to life. Highly recommended!
                                                                                      Mid elem & up

- **Napoleon** - World Leaders Past & Present, by Leslie McGuire
  The World Leaders Past & Present series is unequaled in providing well-researched, well written biographies for young adults. This particular title brings to light some aspects of Napoleon's life that give a broader understanding of why he was considered by much of Europe to be such a tyrant.   **Junior High & up**

- **The Emperor and the Drummer Boy** by Ruth Robbins
  A children's picture book, this is a fascinating anecdote from the life of Napoleon. It permits us an interesting look at one of Napoleon's foibles - his lack of understanding of the sea.
  Elementary

- **The Importance of - Napoleon Bonaparte** by Bob Carroll
  The focus of this children's book is to show both the good and the bad of Napoleon and his quest for power. Throughout the book there are quotes from Napoleon, his biographers and historians which add a tremendous amount of "diagnosis" to the story. Fascinating.
  Upper elem & up

- **Napoleon Bonaparte** - Why They Became Famous Series, by Donnali Shor
  A more advanced "picture book," this is an excellent overview of the main events of Napoleon's life.
  Upper elem & up

- **The Glorious Hussar** by Sir Arthur Conan Doyle
  I couldn't put this book down! It is historical fiction from the viewpoint of an old, retired French soldier who fought under Napoleon and who supposedly figured in many of his escapades. One has to keep reminding oneself that Sir Arthur Conan Doyle was British, not French. We loved it!
  Junior High & up

- **One of the 28th** by G.A. Henty
  Though this title is not currently in print, if you can track it down, you and your students will learn more about the battle of Waterloo and the British soldiers who fought in it than you can imagine! For lovers of battles, this one is a must find. Historical fiction. **Upper elem & up**

- **Waterloo** - Great Battles and Sieges Series, by Philip Sauvain
  An outstanding look at Napoleon's final battle, this book was written and illustrated for children. It is filled with pictures, diagrams, maps, and more. **Upper elem & up**

- **France** - Enchantment of the World Series, by Peter Moss and Thelma Palmer
  This series of books gives a brief overview of the country's history, its geography, and culture. An excellent "primer" for discovering more about France and the French people.
  Mid elem & up

- **Hero of Trafalgar: The Story of Lord Nelson** - A World Landmark Book, by A.B.C. Whipple
  As is true of all of the World Landmark Books, this is an excellent biography for children. Lord Nelson was England's hero and Napoleon's nemesis. Read more about him in this wonderful book!
  Mid elem & up

- **Lord Nelson** - Immortals of History, by Herbert J. Gimpel, Commander, USN
  A very in-depth look at England's most famous admiral, this book also delves into Lord Nelson's "blind spot" - Lady Hamilton.
  Junior High & up

- **Nelson and the Fighting Age of Sail** - A Horizon Caravel Book, by Oliver Warner
  This is an excellent book in the Horizon Caravel series. Lots of illustrations, diagrams, maps, paintings, as well as in-depth text about the man and the strategies he used to defeat Napoleon at sea. Highly recommended!
  Upper elem & up

- **The Navy that Beat Napoleon** - A Cambridge Topic Book, by Walter Brownlee
  For one interested in the sea, this is a must-have! It explained many different aspects of ships-of-the-line and other nautical information that I've not seen anywhere else. Plus, there are easily understood descriptions of the important sea battles which destroyed Napoleon's French fleet. Highly recommended!   **Upper elem & up**

- **The Battle of Trafalgar - Lord Nelson Sweeps the Sea** by Alan Villiers
  An excellent book for children about this greatest and final battle of Lord Nelson. It is truly amazing to realize the genius of Lord Nelson's battle plans and to see the decisive results.
                                                                                              Upper elem & up

- **Two Years Before The Mast** by Richard Henry Dana, Jr.
  While you are reading about Lord Nelson and the British Navy, pick up this true story about a young American who ships out on a sailing vessel in 1840. Classic literature and a can't-put-it down story!   **Junior High & up**

- **The Slave Who Freed Haiti: The Story of Toussaint L'Ouverture** - A World Landmark Book, by Katharine Scherman
  Absolutely fascinating! This is the biography of the "Black Napoleon" who led the successful rebellion against France by the slaves of St. Domingue (Haiti). Highly recommended!
                                                                                              Mid elem and up

- **Toussaint L'Ouverture** - World Leaders Past & Present, by Thomas and Dorothy Hoobler
  This book is an in-depth look at a remarkable man. It shows the developments of France's most successful (read: profitable) colony from the time of the French Revolution through the reign of Napoleon. It was fascinating to read that the National Assembly voted to abolish slavery in France and her colonies, but Napoleon wanted to go back to the prior status quo - so that he could begin reaping the financial benefits of the island! Highly recommended!
                                                                                              Junior High & up

- **The Story of the War of 1812** by Colonel Red Reeder
  In order to better understand the events taking place in Europe in the early 1800's, one must learn more about the war between the U. S. and England/Canada which began in 1812. The seeds of conflict lie deep in the affairs of Napoleon! This is an excellent introduction to the war seen from all sides.   **Upper elem & up**

- **What's the Deal? - Jefferson, Napoleon and the Louisiana Purchase** by Rhoda Blumberg
  This one is worth searching for! I was astonished to learn of Napoleon's interest in North America - and what stopped him. Learn more about how Napoleon swindled the Spanish king for the Louisiana Territory, and how he broke his promise to never sell it to anyone apart from Spain. Fascinating, and highly recommended!   **Upper elem & up**

- **New Orleans** - Battlefields Across America, by David C. King
  This fascinating little book shows us the connection between Andrew Jackson and the British soldiers who were veterans of the Napoleonic Wars. Remember, it's all connected!
                                                                                              Elementary & up

- **Tecumseh - Shawnee Warrior Statesman** by James McCague
  Written for young children, this is an introduction to one of the key players of the War of 1812.
  Elementary & up

- **General Brock and Niagara Falls** - A World Landmark Book, by Samuel Hopkins Adams
  General Brock, an English soldier, first fought against the French forces in Holland, then sailed
  with Lord Nelson to fight the Danes. Hoping to be sent to the Peninsular War in Spain, he was
  instead assigned to Canada. Read more about this hero of the War of 1812 in this excellent
  biography. Highly recommended! **Upper elem & up**

- **Ludwig van Beethoven** - Why They Became Famous Series,
  by Noemi Vicini Marri, translated by Stephen Thorne
  Isn't it amazing to learn that Beethoven composed a symphony (Eroica) in Napoleon's honor?
  And that, when he learned of Napoleon's intention to crown himself as Emperor, Beethoven
  furiously scratched out his name from the music! Learn more about this epoch-shaping
  composer in this excellent biography. **Great Read Aloud**

- **The Life & Times of Beethoven** - Portraits of Greatness Series, by Gino Pugnetti
  This is an excellent overview of the life of the great composer. Filled with paintings,
  illustrations, and more, it describes the many facets and events of Beethoven's life.
  Upper elem & up

- **Touch of Light - The Story of Louis Braille** by Anne E. Neimark
  This is an excellent children's biography of the man who made reading possible for the blind.
  Born in France during the reign of Napoleon, he invented the "Braille" alphabet by the time he
  was fifteen! **Mid elem & up**

- **Louis Braille** by Stephen Keeler
  Filled with drawings and illustrations, this biography of Louis Braille also includes a picture
  and description of the Braille alphabet. **Mid elem & up**

- **Seeing Fingers - The Story of Louis Braille** by Etta DeGering
  Another delightful biography for children. **Mid elem & up**

- **Pride and Prejudice** by Jane Austen
  Wonderful classic literature, this is a story of English society in the early 1800's. It is one of my
  favorite books of all time! **Junior High & up**

- **From Jerusalem to Irian Jaya - A Biographical History of Christian Missions**
  by Ruth A. Tucker
  This is the best book available on the history of world missions. Included are short
  biographies of missionaries all over the world, categorized by their geographical area of
  service. I consider this an indispensable resource for the study of **World Empires, World
  Missions, World Wars**. For this chapter read pages 113 - 138. Highly recommended!
  Upper elem & up

- **Imprisoned in the Golden City** - Trailblazer Books, by Dave & Neta Jackson
  This historical fiction for children presents the story of Adoniram and Ann Judson who went to Burma as missionaries in the early 1800's. **Mid elem & up**

- **William Carey** - Christian Heroes Then and Now, by Janet & Geoff Benge
  Wonderfully written, this series of Christian biographies is fascinating, factual, and historically accurate. William Carey can be considered the "father" of the modern missions movement since it was his willingness to venture out to India in the late 1700's which opened the eyes of many Christians to the possibilities of missions in foreign lands. Highly recommended! **Mid elem & up**

- **William Carey** - Men of Faith Series, by Basil Miller
  This biography was developed from the actual letters and journals of William Carey. It was William Carey's "Expect great things from God; attempt great things for God" that electrified nineteenth century Christians. This book is much more difficult to read than the one listed above, but it has the flavor of an original source document. **Junior High & up**

- **Dates with Destiny - The 100 Most Important Dates in Church History**
  by A. Kenneth Curtis, J. Stephen Lang, and Randy Petersen
  Beginning with the year 64 in Rome and continuing to 1976, this book is filled with short descriptions of events and people within the Church. For this chapter read about William Carey and Adoniram Judson. Highly recommended! **Upper elem & up**

- **The Man Who Freed the Slaves: The Story of William Wilberforce**
  by Audrey Lawson and Herbert Lawson
  This may be difficult to find since it is out-of-print, but it is the only biography written for children that I could find about Wilberforce. He was mightily used by God to end the slave trade in England and her colonies. Highly recommended! **Upper elem & up**

- **William Wilberforce and the Abolition of the Slave Trade** - Christian History, Issue 53
  (Vol. XVI, No. 1)
  This entire edition of Christian History is dedicated to William Wilberforce and the Clapham Community which tremendously impacted England for good in the 1800's. Highly recommended! **Upper elem & up**

- **History of the English-Speaking People, Volume Four** by Winston Churchill
  For an overview of the 1800's, this is an excellent look at the Napoleonic Wars, Great Britain, the British Empire, and the American Civil War. (Churchill has some interesting insights into American history.) **High School & up**

- **Video: War and Peace**
  This video, made during the 1950's and based on Tolstoy's novel, is very long and somewhat depressing. However, it does portray the burning of Moscow during the French invasion, as well as the conditions of battle and the retreat of Napoleon's army during the winter. For me, the most valuable aspect of this movie was seeing Napoleon - he was portrayed magnificently!

Talk Together

Coronation of Napoleon

- Listen to **What in the World's Going On Here?, Volume Two**, Tape One. What did you find to be the most interesting aspect mentioned about Napoleon's life and reign? Why? What other questions about this time period do you have that you would like to have answered? **History Journal:** Write those questions down and, as you study more material, write the answers to your questions. Also, write short bios of the people you study whom you find interesting. Illustrate the bios.

- What words describe Napoleon's rise to power? His reign? Why? Would you consider Napoleon to have had an unusual life? Why or why not? Do you think Napoleon would have risen to power had it not been for the French Revolution? Why or why not? (Hint: Consider the form of government and Napoleon's status prior to the French Revolution.)

- In the conquest of Egypt, what do you think Napoleon's main objectives were? Was he successful in fulfilling these objectives? What were the most significant results of this campaign?

- Imagine you were living in Austria during the time of the Napoleonic Wars. What do you think your impression of Napoleon would be? Contrast that with your impression of him had you been a citizen of France.

- In 1803, Napoleon sold the Louisiana Territory to the U.S. despite his promise to Spain (the former owner) that he would not sell it to anyone. This purchase doubled the size of the U.S.! How do you think the enemies of France viewed this sale? Would they have been for it or against it? Why?

- Why do you think Napoleon was never able to invade England? What are the difficulties involved with invading this island kingdom? What factors came together in 1066 that allowed William of Normandy to be successful in his invasion of England, but which were unavailable to Napoleon? Who else in recent history tried to invade England without success? (Hint: 1940's)

- Many historians point to the Spanish Peninsular War as Napoleon's greatest mistake. Why would this be? Why do you think Napoleon went to war in Spain? Did Napoleon's losses in the Peninsular War impact the rest of Europe? Why or why not?

- The tensions between France and England were demonstrated visibly in the blockade of trade goods from England to the European continent, and in the blockade of imports/exports from the continent to the rest of the world. These tensions led directly to the War of 1812 between the U.S. and England/Canada. How did Napoleon benefit from this war? Did anyone else benefit?

- Napoleon invaded Russia on June 22, 1812, but the Russian army retreated deep into Russia and the peasants followed a "scorched earth" policy as they fled. How did these things impact Napoleon's efforts? How did the Russian winter defeat Napoleon?

- When Napoleon escaped from the island of Elba and returned to France, his enemies frantically prepared for an aggressive war. Why did they do this? Why do you think that at this point, though not before, they labeled Napoleon an outlaw?

- Why is William Carey considered the "Father of Modern Missions"? Describe his life before India and his work in India. What kind of "price" did William Carey have to pay for his time in India? Do you think it was worth it?

- The British and Foreign Bible Society was founded in 1804. What is the impact of having the Bible in your own language? How do you think this society made a difference in the missions work of the Church?

- In 1816, there was the "Réveil," or Awakening, in France under the ministry of Robert Haldane. Why do you think the people of post-Revolutionary, post-Napoleonic France would have been hungry for the things of God? Can you think of other times in history when God has moved mightily among people in deep need?

- William Wilberforce was able, in 1807, to secure passage of a bill in Parliament which outlawed the slavery trade in England and her colonies. Why do you think the English merchants had bitterly fought this bill for years? England was still at war with Napoleon during this time. Do you think there might have been a connection between the passing of this bill and the people's desire to have God's blessing in their fight against Napoleon? Why or why not?

- Toussaint L'Ouverture, though a slave in Haiti, learned to read as a boy. He devoured books on military history which gave him a tremendous preparation for becoming a military leader. The French Revolution granted the slaves under French control freedom, then Napoleon decided to re-enslave them. How do you think this was received by the slaves? Do you see any relation between the slave revolt of Haiti and the outlawing of slavery in England? (Hint: Look at the dates.)

- The Church Missionary Society, founded in 1799, helped to oversee and support missionaries on the field. What factors do you think contributed to the new understanding and new emphasis on world missions among the European and American churches? How would having a society specifically devoted to helping missionaries aid in recruiting new missionaries?

Teaching Time!

Seminar Outline

I. Napoleon (1769 - 1821)
- A. Early life
    1. Born in Corsica
    2. Sent off to military school when ten years old (to France)
- B. Military career
    1. Graduates in "artillery" when he is 16 from Ecole Militaire in Paris
    2. Captain Bonaparte (artillery) & Siege of Toulon - 1793
    3. Promoted to Brigadier General
    4. Temporarily under arrest by Robespierre (Reign of Terror) - 1794
    5. Sent to command Army of Italy - 1796
    6. Captures northern Italy - 1797
    7. Makes treaties not authorized to make
    8. Sends back to Directory millions of dollars worth of "loot"
    9. Egyptian campaign - 1798
    10. Battle of Nile (Lord Nelson)
- C. Political career
    1. Napoleon - First Consul - 1799
    2. Crowns himself Emperor - 1804
    3. Wins Battle of Austerlitz against Austria & Russia - 1805
    4. Invasion of England planned - 1805
        a. Battle of Trafalgar
        b. Lord Nelson dies, but England is victorious
    5. Prussians defeated - 1806
        a. gives rise to German nationalism
        b. gives rise to disciplined Prussian army
    6. Napoleon dissolves Holy Roman Empire - 1806
    7. Russians defeated - 1807
    8. Spanish Peninsular War - 1808
    9. Divorces Josephine - 1809
    10. Marries Marie Louise of Austria
    11. King of Rome born - 1811
    12. Invades Russia with 600,000 men - 1812
    13. Defeated at the Battle of Leipzig - 1813
    14. Napoleon abdicates, sent into exile at Elba - 1814
    15. Hundred Days, Battle of Waterloo - 1815
    16. Exiled to St. Helena in South Atlantic - Dies six years later
- D. Results of Napoleon's reign
    1. To make England the most powerful nation in the world
    2. England exported the gospel of Jesus Christ to the world

II. Revivals and God's Church
- A. England

      1. Baptist Missionary Society founded - 1792
      2. William Carey sails to India - 1793
      3. Church Missionary Society Founded - 1799
      4. British and Foreign Bible Society - 1804
      5. William Wilberforce - Passage of bill outlawing slavery - 1807
  B. America
      1. Beginning of Second Awakening - Early 1800's
      2. Kentucky Revival, "Camp Meetings" - 1801
  C. Scotland
      1. Robert and James Haldane converted - 1795
      2. Under James, renewal in Scotland
  D. France/Switzerland
      1. Robert Haldane - "Réveil (Awakening) - 1816 - 1819
      2. Awakening in France after the devastation of Napoleon
  E. Germany
      1. Revival - Protestant - Early 1800's
      2. Revival - Catholic
  F. Norway
      1. Hans Nielsen Hauge converted - 1786
      2. Begins preaching salvation

IV. Nations around the world
  A. America - third president, Thomas Jefferson, elected - 1800
  B. China - European merchants smuggling opium for trade
  C. India - British East India Company - leading Power
  D. Japan - Completely closed for 200 years, except to Dutch once a year
  E. Ottoman Empire in great decline
      1. Napoleon decimates Egyptian troops
      2. Allows a new person to take control - Muhammed Ali
  F. Prussia -"Absolute Monarchy"
  G. England - "Constitutional Monarchy"

Timeline

On your timeline, mark the rule of Napoleon, the Battle of Trafalgar, Battle of Waterloo, William Carey's life in India, Adoniram Judson in Burma, the Réveil in France and Switzerland.

Research & Reporting

- Find one of the books listed at the beginning of this unit, along with an encyclopedia or other history resource book, for basic information on the Napoleonic Empire. Write a report detailing the rise of Napoleon, his wars, his empire, and his downfall.

- Research and report on the life of Toussaint L'Ouverture. Why was he called the "Black Napoleon"? How unusual was it for Toussaint to know how to read? What were the three different groups of people on this island? Describe Toussaint's battle tactics and their effectiveness.

- Compare and contrast the conditions in Haiti before the French Revolution and after Haitian independence.

- Describe the life and work of Beethoven. How did his childhood experiences and deafness contribute to both his music and his rough personality? Describe Beethoven's attitude toward the French Revolution and Napoleon. How did this change?

- Research and report on the Spanish Peninsular War. Include the tactics of the British under the Duke of Wellington as well as the policy of the French. Describe how the Spanish reacted to having Napoleon's brother on the throne. How did this differ from the reaction of other countries in Europe?

- Write a report on Napoleon's conquest of Egypt, particularly its effect on the study of Egyptology. Include the Rosetta Stone, Jean Paul Champolion, and the impact of the researchers who accompanied Napoleon to Egypt.

- In May, 1804, Napoleon crowned himself Emperor of France. Write a report describing the impact of this Napoleonic Empire on the people of France; his wife, Josephine; the European countries subject to France; the economy of France; and Napoleon himself.

- Study the military genius of Napoleon. Diagram his battles, showing his tactics and how he defeated his enemies. Diagram the battle of Waterloo, showing why he lost, and why the Duke of Wellington thought it was a close call. Describe why Napoleon is considered to have been one of the greatest military minds in history.

- Study the naval genius of Horatio Nelson. Diagram his naval battles, showing how he defeated the French fleet at the Battle of the Nile and the Battle of Trafalgar. Describe why Lord Nelson is considered to be one of the greatest naval tacticians in history.

- Write a report about the War of 1812 comparing and contrasting Napoleon's campaign in Russia with the war between the U.S. and England/Canada. What was the connection between these two wars?

- Research and report on the life and ministry of William Carey. Include information on his background in England, his accomplishments in India, the Serampore Trio, and his tragic family life.

- Adoniram and Ann Judson were among the first American missionaries to go to a foreign field. They traveled to India in 1812, then on to Burma. Write a report on their life and ministry in Burma.

- Research and report on Robert and Mary Moffat, missionaries to Africa in 1816. Robert is considered to be Africa's greatest missionary. Discover why.

- Through the efforts of Robert Morrison in Canton in 1807, the way was essentially paved for future missionaries like Hudson Taylor. Write a report about this first European missionary to China in modern times.

- Research and report on the Clapham Community, of which William Wilberforce was a member. What were the effects of the Clapham Community upon Great Britain? - Upon the world?

- William Wilberforce was the man used by God to abolish the slave trade in Great Britain. Research and report on this man, his life's work, and the abolitionist movements in different parts of the world. (Hint: Include Haiti, Jamaica, the U.S., etc.)

- Study Louis Braille and the Braille alphabet. Report on the ways that the Braille alphabet has helped the blind, and how blind people may access information in Braille today.

 **Brain Stretchers**

- Napoleon, in his exile to St. Helena, remarked that his best work, and what the world would remember about him, was the Napoleonic Code of Law. Research and report on this, including the prior history of law in France, the implementation of the Napoleonic Code throughout the French-speaking world, and some of the most significant aspects of the Code.

- Napoleon has been called "The Father of Modern Germany." Research and report on the impact of Napoleon's actions in the Holy Roman Empire, the Confederation of the Rhine, and the defeat of the Prussians.

Vocabulary

despotism	abolition	absolute monarchy	constitutional monarchy
nepotism	Braille	ships-of-the-line	campaign (military use)
blockade	artillery	"scorched earth" policy	society (as in "Bible Society")
abdication	exile	Napoleonic Code	tactician

In this unit there is a great emphasis on military terminology - for the army and for the navy.

- Your assignment is to collect as many military terms as you find in this unit's study and define them.

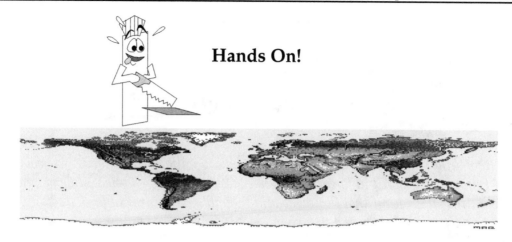

Hands On!

Maps and Mapping

- Using an atlas, encyclopedia, or other resource locate Corsica, France, Haiti, Burma, India, Serampore, Trafalgar, Waterloo, the English Channel, Elba, St. Helena, Louisiana Purchase (the land area included in Napoleon's sale to the U.S.), and the site of the Peninsular War.

- What are the names of the cities and countries that today occupy the same areas? What is the capital city, religion, population, major export, and type of government in each modern country? What is the status of Christianity in these countries?

- On a clean worksheet map, draw lines tracing the route of Napoleon's various armies, marking their historic battles and which of the battles were successful. On the same map, indicate the Napoleonic Empire at its height. Mark Napoleon's small kingdom of Elba, the place of his final demise.

- On a separate map, show the places in India where William Carey lived and ministered. Be sure to show which areas were under the jurisdiction of the British East India Company, which were under the Dutch East India Company, and which were ruled independently by Indian princes. Locate Burma and show the area where Adoniram Judson ministered.

- Consult a relief map to discover the terrain encountered in the Napoleonic Wars. Are there deserts, forest, mountains, islands? Label them. What kind of climate is typical in each of the different terrains? How did these different terrains and climates effect Napoleon's armies (especially in Egypt and Russia)?

- Consult a relief map to discover the terrain found in India. Are there deserts, forest, mountains, islands? Label them. What kind of climate is typical in each of the different terrains? How did these different terrains and climates effect the missionaries who came to share the Gospel with the Indian people?

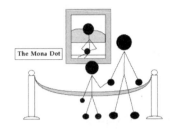

The Mona Dot

Art Appreciation

The French Revolution and the reign of Napoleon had a dramatic effect upon art, especially on the continent of Europe. It ushered in "neoclassicism" - a return to the classical style of ancient Rome and Greece. In painting, this meant that figures would resemble sculptures in form and simplicity, objects would have very defined outlines, and that colors would be kept to a minimum (though bright colors could be used).

The court painter for Napoleon was Jean Louis David (1748 - 1825). He painted both historic scenes from Rome and Greece as well as contemporary people and events. His paintings prior to the French Revolution were often politically explosive, inflaming the revolutionary ardor of the people.

- Locate David's painting, "Napoleon Crossing the Great St. Bernard Pass." Would you describe this painting as realistic? Why or why not? What message about Napoleon do you think David wanted to convey in this portrait?

- In the article on Painting in the **World Book Encyclopedia** you will see David's painting, "The Oath of the Horatii." It shows the sacrifice willingly made by three brothers for the sake of the Rxoman Republic. Painted in 1784, during the years building up to the French Revolution, this painting had a dramatic effect upon the French people. Why do you suppose this was so effective? What kind of effect do you think David intended? How might this have helped lead to the Revolution?

Francisco de Goya (1746 - 1828), the great Spanish painter, completely rejected the Neo-Classical style of painting by returning to the Baroque form of art, foreshadowing the Romantic style of painting. Goya's art is emotional, imaginative, fluid, using color and shadow, and often filled with horrors. He was a court painter for Spain until the King of Spain abdicated and Napoleon sent his armies to take over. The people of Spain resisted Napoleon, and Goya captured the resulting tragedies on canvas.

- Find Goya's "King Charles IV of Spain and his Family," to see his style of painting portraits. Do you think he painted flattering pictures? Would you describe this as realistic? Would you have wanted Goya to paint your portrait?

- "The Third of May, 1808" is one of Goya's most powerful paintings. It shows Napoleon's army carrying out retribution for the actions of a few rebellious Spaniards - 5,000 people were executed. How would you describe this painting? How is it different from David's painting of Napoleon?

Arts in Action

- Try your hand at creating Neo-Classical art. You may wish to draw, paint, use modeling clay, or Legos. Create a backdrop with simple Greek or Roman columns, stairs, marble flooring, etc. Add a few subjects, dramatically posed. Compose a title such as, "Dianacus awaiting inspiration." Have fun!

- Choose an adventure from your life (or one of your family members). Create a stylized depiction of the adventure, showing the heroic nature of the central character. This is not an exercise in realism, it is to emphasize the dramatic nature of the event, similar to David's painting of Napoleon crossing the Alps. Be inspired!

Architecture

"... OOPS!! ..."

The Neo-Classical style was also evident in architecture beginning in the mid-1700's and continuing into the 1800's. This was due in part to the excavations at Pompeii and Herculaneum which provided architects with excellent models of Roman architecture.

In England, the beginning of the 1800's ushered in the Regency Period - a revival of Greek style. The main architects of this time were Sir John Soane and John Nash. Since Mr. Nash was patronized by George IV, his works are more extensive and better known. Perhaps his most famous architectural design was Regent's Park in London.

- Look for a photo of the Pantheon in Paris, designed by Jacques-Germain Soufflot. This is an excellent representation of Neo-Classicist architecture.

- Look up Architecture in an encyclopedia for another example of Neo-Classical architecture (such as the Syon House near London, designed by Robert Adam).

Science

Georges Cuvier (1769-1832) was a scientist in France during the time of the Revolution, Napoleon and the "Restoration" (when the Bourbon kings regained the throne). He is best remembered for his work in establishing the sciences of comparative anatomy and paleontology (the study of fossil remains). He maintained that the fossil record showed clearly the reality of Creation (no in-between species) and refuted the notion of evolution.

- Visit a fossil! Natural history museums, plaeontological digs, zoos, and fossil shops all have interesting fossil specimens to examine. Ask yourself these questions: Is this a marine animal, land animal or plant? Is it extinct? Is it an unusual fossil? Why or why not? Where was it found? (**Dry Bones and Other Fossils** by Dr. Gary Parker is an excellent introduction to fossils for younger students. **Buried Alive** by Dr. Jack Cuozo, for advanced students, is an amazing exposé of paleontological practices by modern evolutionist scientists.)

 # Music

The music of Ludwig van Beethoven predominates during the early 1800's - the Napoleonic era. He actually dedicated his third symphony to Napoleon - until he learned that his "hero of humanity" had crowned himself Emperor!

Beethoven's music is the bridge between the Classical style of music (Haydn, Mozart) and the Romantics (Schubert, Berlioz, Mendelssohn, Schumann, Liszt, Chopin, etc.). Just as the Neo-Classicist movement in painting and architecture (with its emphasis on form, simplicity, and control) gave way to Romanticism and Realism (with emotion, imagination, lack of restraint) so Beethoven's music moves from Classical to Romantic.

- Listen to Beethoven's Fifth Symphony. In its form, it is similar to the symphonies of the classical era, but the emotion that is displayed in the way he works with his famous theme - "da da da DAAA ....." - is indicative of what is to come in the Romantic era.

Cooking

This recipe was created by Napoleon's chef after Napoleon's great victory at the battle of Marengo!

Chicken Marengo

1/2 cup flour
1 tsp. salt
1/2 tsp black pepper
1 tsp. dried tarragon
3 lbs. chicken, cut in pieces
1/4 cup olive oil

1/4 cup butter
1 cup dry white wine
2 cups canned tomatoes
1 clove garlic, finely chopped
10 mushrooms, sliced

Preheat oven to 350 degrees. Mix flour, salt, pepper, and tarragon, then dredge chicken pieces in this mixture. In a frying pan, heat the olive oil and butter together. When it is sufficiently hot, brown the chicken on all sides. Place the chicken in a heavy casserole dish. Whisk the remaining flour mixture into the oil and butter until smooth, gradually add wine until sauce is thickened and smooth. Pour it over the chicken, add the tomatoes, garlic and mushrooms. Cover casserole with an ovenproof lid, and bake until chicken is tender (about 45 minutes.) If you would like, sprinkle fresh parsley over the chicken just before serving. Serves 6.

Be sure to serve with french bread and a salad. Bon Appetit!

Idea Time

Creative Writing

- As a reporter for the "Island Insider," interview Toussaint L'Ouverture to discover why the slaves of Haiti have rebelled. Analyze his chances of holding out against the Napoleonic Empire. What does he have working for him? What does he have working against him? Next, interview William Wilberforce to find his views on the importance of the abolition of slavery.

- Write a job application to William Carey or Adoniram Judson. Tell them why you would like to work alongside them in ministry, how your skills and/or experience would qualify you, being careful to display your familiarity with the work they have accomplished in India and Burma.

- Write a letter to the editor of the "Empire Herald" expressing your views of Napoleon's decision to divorce Josephine and marry Marie Louise. Are you outraged? Tell why, but remember to couch it in such a way that it does not provoke the Imperial temper!

- You are the King of Spain. When you turned over the Louisiana Territory in the Americas to Napoleon, you required that he promise to never give it to anyone else unless he returned it to you. You just learned that he SOLD it to Thomas Jefferson of the United States. Write Napoleon your thoughts - in courteous and formal language, of course. Be sure to remind him of your former agreement.

 **Art**

- Draw a political cartoon of Napoleon's exile on Elba. Remember that he didn't stay long - it was much too small of a kingdom!

Drama

- Dramatize the War of 1812 - in Russia. Half of your actors should play the part of the French army (which was smug going into Russia) and the other half should play the part of the Russian peasants (who were smug when the Russian winter destroyed the French). Remember that Napoleon makes it to safety in his comfortable coach.

- Act out William Carey's early life - from shoemaker's apprentice to a fledgling missionary to India.

The Big Picture

- While Napoleon sought to establish an empire for himself, William Carey sought to establish the Kingdom of God in India. Decide how to best show the differences between these two men, sharing the effects of their lives and work with your family, friends, and neighbors.

Unit 2

Industrialization & The Church's Response, Nationalism & The Crimean War

Castle of Chapuleptec

Unit Objectives:

- To discover the circumstances leading up to the Industrial Revolution, and to observe its impact upon people, economics, and science;

- to see how George Muller was used of God to care for the orphans of the Industrial Revolution, and to contrast this with Charles Dickens' novels about industrialized England;

- to learn about the Second Awakening in America, Charles Finney, and revivals in the 1800's throughout the world;

- to study Commodore Perry and his black ships in Japan;

- to read about the struggles for independence in South America, Mexico and Italy;

- to understand the Crimean War, and the impact Florence Nightingale had upon the nursing field.

Meet the People & Study the Countries:

Here are some people you might meet in this unit:

In the Church:

George Muller	Elizabeth Fry	Lord Shaftsbury
Charles Finney	Florence Nightingale	

In the World:

James Watt	Robert Fulton	Samuel Morse
Commodore Perry	Michael Faraday	Charles Dickens
Simon Bolivar	Garibaldi	Klemens von Metternich
Emperor Maximillian	Benito Juarez	

You might wish to study one of these places in depth during this unit:

England	Japan (also in Units 5 and 8)	The Crimea
Mexico	South America	Italy

- **The Holy Bible**
  Proverbs 14:21, 22:22, 25:2; Isaiah 58:6-11; Luke 6:38; Galatians 2:10

- **James Watt - The Man who Transformed the World** by William D. Crane
  James Watt was the man who perfected the steam engine which brought about the Industrial Revolution. This fascinating biography gives many of the details of his life and inventions - including the fact that he was homeschooled! Highly recommended! **Upper elem & up**

- **Inventors of the World** by I.O. Evans
  This is a delightful children's book presenting short biographies about several inventors. It includes the Morse code that Samuel Morse developed. **Upper elem & up**

- **Scientists Who Changed The World** - Turning Points in History Series,
  by Philip Wilkinson and Michael Pollard
  Apart from the article on Charles Darwin, I found this to be a wonderful book about scientists. There are lots of pictures, "fascinating facts," a timeline, and more. **Mid elem & up**

- **Watt Got You Started, Mr. Fulton? - A Story of James Watt & Robert Fulton**
  by Robert Quackenbush
  This interesting little book contains lots of information about these two pioneers of the Industrial Revolution. Did you know that Robert Fulton tried to interest Napoleon in his submarine, the Nautilus? Highly recommended! **Elementary & up**

- **The Industrial Revolution Begins** - A Cambridge Topic Book, by Christine Vialls
  For those who want to know how the Industrial Revolution began, this excellent book covers it from the early days of smelting cast iron with charcoal in England to the changes which took place when manufacturers began making steel. Fascinating! **Upper elem & up**

- **Power for the People** - The Cambridge Introduction to History Series, by Trevor Cairns
  This is an excellent overview of the 1800's. It incorporates both the intellectual climate (with philosophers, writers, musicians, and artists) and the political climate (with the changing European power structures). I found this book to be one of the very best in describing the transitions from one event to the next during this time frame. (Parents: There are three objectionable pictures in this book. Please make your own decision.)   **Upper elem & up**

- **Boat Builder** by Clara Ingram Judson
  This is a younger children's biography of Robert Fulton. I found it especially captivating in the description of Fulton's submarine - the Nautilus.   **Elementary & up**

- **Samuel Slater's Mill and The Industrial Revolution** - Turning Points in American History, by Christopher Simonds
  "Since 1774, it had been illegal to send textile machinery, or the plans for it, out of England." And so is told the pivotal experience of the first Englishman to smuggle plans out of England (in his head!) for the construction of cotton-spinning machines. Thus was born the Industrial Revolution in America!   **Mid elem & up**

- **A Head Full of Notions - A Story about Robert Fulton** by Andy Russell Bowen
  A well-written, interesting biography of Robert Fulton. It was fascinating to learn that he did not enjoy school, since, "My head is so full of original notions that there is no vacant chamber to store away the contents of dusty books." Amen to that.   **Mid elem & up**

- **Nineteenth-Century Inventors** - American Profiles, by Jon Noonan
  Though this book focuses on American inventors, the inventions of Robert Fulton, Samuel F.B. Morse, Thomas Edison, Alexander Graham Bell and others changed the world. Fascinating!   **Upper elem & up**

- **Smithsonian Visual Timeline of Inventions** by Richard Platt
  The second half of this book deals with inventions in the 1800's and 1900's. Wonderful pictures and short descriptions make this a great book to set out for your students!   **Mid elem & up**

- **Men of Science, Men of Invention** - American Heritage Jr. Library, by Michael Blow
  Learn about the Industrial Revolution in America, the impact of the development of internal combustion on machines and people, the attempts of Edison to develop a light bulb (lamp), and splitting the atom (both for good and for destructive purposes). This book will provide an excellent overview of the scientific developments of the 1800's and early 1900's. Highly recommended!   **Upper elem and up**

- **21 Great Scientists Who Believed the Bible** by Ann Lamont
  From Johannes Kepler to Wernher von Braun, this book of short biographies is an excellent addition to the study of **World Empires, World Missions, World Wars**. The biographies are longer and much more in depth than **Men of Science, Men of God**. Highly recommended!   **Upper elem & up**

- **Men of Science, Men of God - Great Scientists Who Believed the Bible** by Henry M. Morris
101 short biographies of scientists who were either Christians or believed in the Judeo Christian worldview. There is just enough here to whet your appetite. Excellent!
Upper elem & up

- **The Thieves of Tyburn Square** - Trailblazer Books, by Dave & Neta Jackson
Historical fiction for children, this title describes the work of Elizabeth Fry to reform the penal system in England. Highly recommended! **Mid elem & up**

- **The Bandit of Ashley Downs** - Trailblazer Books, by Dave & Neta Jackson
Historical fiction for children, this title describes the ministry of George Muller to orphans in England during the mid-1800's. Highly recommended! **Mid elem & up**

- **Dates with Destiny - The 100 Most Important Dates in Church History**
by A. Kenneth Curtis, J. Stephen Lang, and Randy Petersen
Beginning with the year 64 in Rome and continuing to 1976, this book is filled with short descriptions of events and people within the Church. For this chapter, read the articles on William Wilberforce, Elizabeth Fry and Charles Finney. Highly recommended!
Upper elem & up

- **George Muller** - Christian Heroes Then and Now, by Janet & Geoff Benge
Wonderfully written, this series of Christian biographies is fascinating, factual, and historically accurate. George Muller was the man who believed God was able to provide all the needs for orphan houses. He ministered to the orphans of the Industrial Revolution at the same time that Charles Dickens wrote Oliver Twist. Highly recommended! **Upper elem & up**

- **George Muller: Man of Faith and Miracles** - Men of Faith Series, by Basil Miller
This biography is filled with quotes from Mr. Muller's journals, along with the insights to help us understand what was taking place through his ministry. Highly recommended!
Junior High & up

- **The Autobiography of George Muller** by George Muller
This is an amazing, detailed recounting of God's faithfulness in answer to Mr. Muller's prayers. Life-changing! **Junior High & up**

- **Johann Sebastian Bach had a Wife** by William J. Petersen
This is a delightful collection of stories about famous couples, including George and Mary Muller. **Junior High & up**

- **Charles Dickens - The Man Who Had Great Expectations** by Diane Stanley & Peter Venema
I love Diane Stanley's books! Her illustrations are wonderful, and the biography is well told. This is the story of Charles Dickens and his life. Highly recommended! **Great Read Aloud**

- **Charles Dickens - His Life** by Catherine Owens Peare
Charles Dickens was one of the most widely read authors in Victorian England. Read about his life - his successes and his failures - in this excellent biography. **Upper elem & up**

- **Oliver Twist** by Charles Dickens
  This book of classic literature is one of the great depictions of life in early industrialized Great Britain. If the book is too difficult, watch the movie or the musical, **Oliver**.
  Junior High & up

- **Charles Finney** - Men of Faith Series, by Basil Miller
  Published by Bethany House, these Men of Faith and Women of Faith biographies are excellent. This title tells the story of Charles Finney and his prayer partner, Father Nash.
  Fascinating! **Junior High & up**

- **Commodore Perry In Japan** - American Heritage Jr. Library by Robert L. Reynolds
  The story is well told in this interesting book of the "black ships" from America that went to Japan in 1853 and forced open the door of trade which had been closed for two centuries.
  Highly recommended! **Upper elem & up**

- **Florence Nightingale** - Why They Became Famous, by Donnali Shor
  What a fantastic book! Learn about Florence Nightingale's childhood - including the time when her family fled Switzerland during a European tour because Louis Napoleon (soon to be Napoleon III) had sought refuge there; about her heroic work during the Crimean War; about her incredible influence in the medical field and in many reforms of the British Army. Highly recommended! **Mid elem & up**

- **Florence Nightingale** - A World Landmark Book, by Ruth Fox Hume
  As is the case with all of the World Landmark Books, this biography is an excellent look at its subject, this time the "Angel of the Crimea." Highly recommended! **Upper elem & up**

- **Florence Nightingale** by Jeannette Covert Nolan
  Written more in the form of a story, this is a very interesting biography of one of the world's greatest champions for the destitute and underprivileged. **Upper elem & up**

- **Florence Nightingale: The Lady of the Lamp** - Women of Faith Series, by Basil Miller
  This biography focuses the reader's attention upon the Christian foundation that was Florence Nightingale's motivation for her sacrificial life. Though it is more difficult to read, Christians will appreciate the specific look at her faith in Jesus Christ. **Junior High & up**

- **Klemens von Metternich** - World Leaders Past & Present, by John von der Heide
  A biography of the Austrian architect of Europe after the fall of Napoleon, this book is absolutely a "must read." It was von Metternich's philosophy of government that ruled in Europe until 1848 - the year of revolutions. Critical to your understanding of this era!
  Junior High and up

- **Simon Bolivar** - World Leaders Past & Present, by Dennis Wepman
  Considered to be the "George Washington" of South America, Simon Bolivar was a man who never gave up. This is an excellent biography of the man who liberated South America, almost singlehandedly, from Spain. **Junior High & up**

- **Simon Bolivar: The Great Liberator** - A World Landmark Book, by Arnold Whitridge
This is an excellent introduction to one of the most important figures in South American history. It is very readable, very interesting. Highly recommended!   **Mid elem & up**

- **Garibaldi: Father of Modern Italy** - A World Landmark Book, by Marcia Davenport
Did you know that Italy had not been united as one country since the time of the Roman Empire until 1870? This is a biography of the man who led his country to independence and unity against the great powers of Europe. Well-written and fascinating to read! Highly recommended!   **Upper elem & up**

- **Giuseppe Garibaldi** - World Leaders Past & Present, by Herman J. Viola and Susan P. Viola
Garibaldi lived a life of adventure and danger with the purpose of seeing his country freed from foreign rule. This excellent book shows the many facets of his life and work.
Junior High & up

- **Ashes of Empire - Carlota and Maximilian of Mexico** by Marguerite Vance
The story of the Emperor and Empress of Mexico from 1864-1867, this book sympathetically describes the tragedy of this royal couple.   **Upper elem & up**

- **The Execution of Maximilian - June 19, 1867:**
A Hapsburg Emperor Meets Disaster in the New World by Robin McKown
Straightforward and factual, this children's book gives the basic overview of France's attempt to set up a colonial empire in Mexico with a Hapsburg as emperor. I found it to have the clearest explanation of the reasons both for France's involvement in and departure from Mexico. Highly recommended!   **Upper elem & up**

- **Juarez, The Founder of Modern Mexico** by Ronald Syme
This is a fascinating story of the first Zapotec Indian to become President of Mexico. He fled to the U.S. when Maximilian came as Emperor, but returned at his downfall. Highly recommended!   **Upper elem & up**

- **Juarez - Man of Law** by Elizabeth Borton de Trevino
Another excellent biography of Juarez, focusing on his commitment to the law. The author writes, "He is regarded as a hero because he was stubbornly devoted to the idea that strict observance of the law is what makes men worthy, that law is the greatest achievement of men in their efforts to live together peacefully on this earth, and that justice must be the same for everyone."   **Upper elem & up**

- **The French Foreign Legion** - A World Landmark Book, by Wyatt Blassingame
Created in 1832 by King Louis Philippe of France, the French Foreign Legion played a significant part in many wars around the globe, including the attempt to conquer Mexico, WWI, and WWII. Highly recommended!   **Upper elem & up**

- **Video - Oliver**
This musical presentation of Dickens' **Oliver Twist** is memorable. There are some scary people (at least, they scared me!), so parents may want to preview this before allowing their younger children to watch it.

Talk Together

Napoleon III

- Listen to **What in the World's Going On Here?, Volume Two**, Tape One - Side Two. What were the most interesting aspects to you of the Industrial Revolution, George Muller's orphanages, Charles Finney, or Europe in the mid-1800's? Why? What other questions about this time period would you like to have answered?
  History Journal: Write those questions down and, as you study more material, write the answers to your questions. Also, write short bios of the people you study whom you find interesting. Illustrate the bios.

- Why was the steam engine such a vital part of the Industrial Revolution? What uses did people find for the steam engine? If you had been alive when James Watt introduced his improved steam engine, do you think you would have been glad for the power it provided? Why or why not? If your parents or your uncles and aunts had been living at the onset of the Industrial Revolution, how would their jobs have been affected?

- At the beginning of the Industrial Revolution, canals had to be built in order to transport heavy, large quantities of materials to and from factories. Why do you suppose factories were not built right next to the supply of raw materials? Why didn't they just use the existing rivers for transportation? How difficult do you suppose it was to build a canal? What was involved?

- Why was Britain known as the "workshop of the world"? How were Britain's colonies instrumental in making Britain this workshop? Who supplied the investment capital (money) that was used to build the factories?

- Many poor farmers began to come to the industrial areas looking for work as their harvests failed, or as it became impossible to make a living on the farm. Imagine you were part of a farm family that moved to one of the "big" cities in industrialized England. Describe your living conditions. Describe your working conditions. Explain why slums developed in these areas.

- George Muller was burdened for the orphans of industrialized England. Why did he say that he wanted to trust in God alone for the support of the five orphan houses? Do you think that God's miraculous provisions for the orphans made an impact on the people of Bristol? Why or why not? If you had been an orphan living at one of Mr. Muller's orphanages, how would you have felt when one of these miracles occurred?

- There is a story told on the tape about Charles Finney going into a textile mill. Why do you think his looking at a girl caused her to start weeping? Why did the others join in? Would it be unusual today for a factory manager to shut down the factory so the workers could "attend to their souls"? Explain.

- The year 1848 was known as a year of revolutions across Europe. Why do you think the monarchs worked very hard to quell these revolutions? Some of the monarchs used force, others agreed to make concessions in order to slow down the revolutionary fervor. What do you think would have more impact - the better possibility of working - between these two approaches? Why?

- Napoleon III was originally brought to power by the vote of the people of France. Do you think his name and relation to Napoleon Bonaparte had anything to do with his election? Can you think of any other people in politics who are elected because of their name and family relations? Would you consider it wise to elect someone for this reason? Why or why not?

- The Crimean War brought together armies from the Ottoman Empire, France and England on one side, and Russia on the other. Why do you think that France and England would join forces with the Muslim Ottomans against the Orthodox Russians? What does "balance of power" mean? How does it apply to this war? Who won? What impact did the war have on the winner? On the loser?

- Imagine that you belonged to Florence Nightingale's social group. What would you think of the news that she was leaving to nurse the wounded in the Crimea? Why would this have been considered so shocking? Is there any place or activity that a young person could pursue today that would be similarly shocking? How did Florence Nightingale effect the nursing profession? How did the work in the Crimea effect her?

- Do you think Commodore Perry had a positive impact on Japan? Why or why not? What did the Japanese think of Commodore Perry? What were the results of his visit?

- Simon Bolivar was considered to be the George Washington of South America. Why? Why did Spain let go of her colonies? What influence did Napoleon have on this?

- Garibaldi was an Italian patriot who desired to see his country united instead of parceled out to many rulers. He seemed to be a "larger than life" figure to many of his countrymen. Why? How did his work in Venezuela impact this? How successful was he?

- Why do you think Napoleon III wanted to find a monarch for Mexico? What good would it do him? Why do you think Maximillian was chosen? What did the population of Mexico think of Maximillian? Do you think he knew? Why or why not? Why do you think Juarez allowed Maximillian to be executed?

Teaching Time!

Seminar Outline

I. Industrialization
   A. Began in England
      1. Steam engine - reliable power - James Watt - 1775
      2. Canal system, then railroads - reliable transportation
      3. Britain - "The workshop of the world"
   B. Change from agriculture/handcrafted system to factories
      1. Capital, power, labor under one roof
      2. Created slums - no source of transportation out to suburbs!
   C. Poor farmers become poor laborers
      1. When farm fails, go to cities for work
      2. Live in slum conditions
      3. Long hours
      4. Low wages
      5. Children working
   D. Four C's of Industrial Revolution:
      1. Coal Mining
         a. to smelt iron (then steel)
         b. to make steam for machines
      2. Canals
         a. for barges to carry raw materials
         b. for barges to carry finished goods
      3. Capital
         a. London - Commerce Capital of the World
         b. Profits from colonies to invest
      4. Cheap labor
         a. Poor farm workers flock to city
         b. Increasing work force

II. Impact of Industrial Revolution in human suffering
   A. Charles Dickens
      1. **Oliver Twist** published serially 1837 - 1839
      2. Wrote about the problems in the British industrial society
   B. George Muller (1805 - 1898)
      1. Born in Prussia, becomes British Citizen
      2. Converted - 1825
      3. Comes to London - 1829
      4. Began Orphan Houses - 1835
         a. Where orphans were fed and clothed by God, through prayer
         b. Where facilities were maintained through prayer
      5. Eventually 2,000 orphans in five great houses, all by prayer!

III. Second Awakening in America
    A. Charles Finney (1792-1875)
        1. Father of Modern Revivalism
        2. Preached across America - Second Awakening
        3. Based on prayer and fasting

IV. The Mid-1800's
    A. 1848 - The Year of Revolutions in Europe
    B. France
        1. Napoleon III comes to power
        2. 2nd Empire
    C. Crimean War - 1853
        1. Britain, France, Turkey, Russia
        2. Florence Nightingale
            a. Born in Florence, Italy, to a wealthy, upper class British family
            b. Women of her culture not suited to nursing
            c. She was called of God!
            d. Kaiserwerth (Prussia)
    D. Prussia
        1. Prussia defeats Austria in 1866
        2. Prussia sets up North German Confederation
    E. America - Commodore Perry sails for Japan - 1853
    F. India - Rebellion in 1857; 1858 placed under British Government Rule
    G. Italy - becomes Kingdom of Italy, 1861 (nationalism)
    H. American Civil War - 1861-1865
        1. More than 600,000 die
        2. In the South - State's Rights
        3. In the North - Abolish Slavery
        4. South provides cotton for Europe
        5. North provides wheat for Europe

Timeline

On your timeline, mark the invention of the steam engine, Charles Dickens, George Muller, Charles Finney, Elizabeth Fry, Lord Shaftsbury, Napoleon III, Florence Nightingale, the Year of Revolutions, Commodore Perry, Garibaldi, Maximillian, Juarez, von Metternich, and the American Civil War.

Research & Reporting

- Find one of the books listed at the beginning of this unit, along with the encyclopedia or other history resource book, for basic information on the Industrial Revolution. Write a report explaining the "Four C's" required for the Industrial Revolution to happen.

- Investigate living conditions among the poor in the early 1800's in England. Make a chart showing what the conditions were, what caused them, and who improved them. (Elizabeth Fry and Lord Shaftsbury are important people to consider for this report.)

- Research and report on James Watt and/or Robert Fulton. Describe their early lives, their scientific inventions, where they secured funding for their research, the public reception to these inventions, and how these inventions changed the world.

- Robert Fulton demonstrated his Nautilus, the first submarine, to Napoleon in 1801. Napoleon was not interested. Research and report on the Nautilus and on the growth and development of submarines as weapons of war.

- Study and write on the life of George Muller. Show his childhood, his life before Christ, and his ministry. Describe his careful accounting and his careful recording of God's provision through the years. Give examples of this. Describe his method of dealing with difficulties. Give examples. Describe the accomplishments of his final twenty years?

- Research and report on Charles Finney and the Second Awakening in America. Finney is described as the "Father of Revivalism." What does that mean? What was the basis for Finney's ministry? Describe Father Nash and his importance to Finney. Describe the effect Finney had upon the towns he visited.

- In 1857, a noon prayer meeting was begun in New York City. The result of this ongoing prayer meeting was revival. Research and report on this revival and on the Irish Revival of 1859. (The book, **Revival Fire**, by Wesley Duewel, will be an excellent resource for much of this information.)

- Research and report on Klemens von Metternich of Austria. Describe the Congress of Vienna in 1814-1815. What was Metternich's policy? How did this policy influence the monarchs of Europe and Russia? What was Metternich's policy towards Italy? What caused Metternich's influence to end? Define and analyze "The Age of Metternich."

- In Europe, the year 1848 was known as the Year of Revolutions. Study and write about the various cities that were involved in these revolutions. What was the effect of revolution in each of these cities/countries? Compare and contrast these revolutions to the American Revolution of 1776, the French Revolution of 1789, and the Communist Revolution of 1917.

- Study the military strategies of the Crimean War. What did Napoleon III introduce into naval warfare? How did the Industrial Revolution effect the Crimean War? What were the tactics of the war, and what results did they produce? What was the overall impact of the Crimean War upon Russia? - Upon the Ottoman Empire? - Upon France? - Upon England?

- Research and report on the life of Florence Nightingale. Describe the state of nursing in England prior to Florence Nightingale's involvement and the changes that took place as a result of her influence.

- Research and report on Simon Bolivar. Why was he called the "George Washington" of South America? How did Bolivar wrest South America from Spain? What event in Napoleonic Europe contributed to this? What countries did Bolivar "liberate"? What countries did Bolivar govern? What happened to these countries after the death of Bolivar?

- Study and write about the history of Mexico from the time of independence from Spain through the reform government of Benito Juarez. Describe the Empire of Mexico under Maximillian - how it rose and how it fell. Write about the life of Benito Juarez and his political policies. How did they change Mexico?

- Research and report on the life of Giuseppi Garibaldi and the struggle for the unification of Italy. Describe the political division in Italy. Show which European countries governed the different parts of Italy prior to the unification.

- Research and report on the effect the American Civil War had in Europe, and on ways that the outcome of the war was effected by policies of the various European countries.

Brain Stretchers

- Research and report on Napoleon III. What political theory did he follow? Who was Saint-Simon and what were his theories? How did the Second Republic become the Second Empire? Analyze the factors leading to success in the Second Empire, and the factors leading to its downfall. What part did Napoleon III play in the Crimean War? - In Maximillian's empire in Mexico?

- Describe Florence Nightingale's effect upon military policy in England, the Red Cross, and hospitals throughout the world. Analyze how Christianity made a difference both in Florence Nightingale's work and in the nursing profession.

- Research and report on the increase of Prussian strength and influence in German affairs, and the decrease of Austrian influence. What was the Seven Weeks' War between Prussia and Austria? What was the result of this war? Describe the North German Confederation. How did this differ from the German Confederation?

Vocabulary

mechanization	industrialized	nursing	inventions
charcoal	smelting	manufacture	textiles
orphanage	status quo	censorship	canals
workshop	slum	urbanization	concession
repression	confederation	liberate	

In this unit there is a great emphasis on the terminology of the Industrial Revolution and of Nationalism.

- Your assignment is to collect as many terms as you find in this unit's study on either industrialization or nationalism, then define them.

Hands On!

**Maps
and
Mapping**

- Using an atlas, encyclopedia, or other resource locate London (the "workshop of the world"), Japan, Mexico, Italy, Bolivia, Colombia, Ecuador, Peru, Venezuela, and the Crimean Peninsula.

- What are the names of the cities and countries that today occupy the same areas? What is the capital city, religion, population, major export, and type of government in each modern country? What is the status of Christianity in these countries?

- On a clean worksheet map of the world, draw lines tracing Commodore Perry's trip to Japan. Also, using separate colors for each, shade the area which Simon Bolivar liberated, Giuseppe Garibaldi fought for, Maximilian and Juarez fought over, and the area of the Crimean War (labeling the various countries involved in this war).

- Consult a relief map to discover the terrain found in the Crimea, as well as the areas of nationalism studied in this unit (South America, Mexico, Italy, Japan). Are there deserts, forest, mountains, islands? Label them. What kind of climate is typical in each of the different terrains? How did these different terrains and climates effect the combatants fighting to win wars and liberate nations?

The City of Mexico

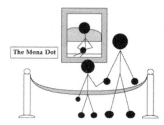

Art Appreciation

In reaction to the strict, controlled forms of Neo-Classicism, many artists, poets, architects and musicians sought a more expressive, emotional, free-flowing style of art - Romanticism. In painting, this was expressed in luxurious use of color, less defined outlines of objects (sometimes objects are barely recognizable because of the indistinct, hazy outline), an emphasis on nature and simple, homey scenes (rather than Roman or Greek history), and the use of shadows and lights.

In England, the two most important painters of this time period were Joseph Turner and John Constable. Turner was the master at marine paintings while Constable was the master of English landscape. Art historians have compared these artists to the poetry of Lord Byron and William Wordsworth - Turner with his turbulent seascapes shows the same feeling towards nature's destructive power that Lord Byron expresses in "Childe Harold," while Constable with his gentle, soothing landscapes reflects Wordsworth's comforting view of nature.

Joseph Turner created paintings in many different styles, including lovely landscapes, fierce storms, and studies in lighting. Many of his later works were not appreciated by the audience of his day but are highly esteemed today.

- Find Turner's painting, "The Shipwreck" and/or his painting, "Snowstorm: Hannibal and His Army Crossing the Alps." How would you describe these paintings? How do they fit the description of the Romantic style? In **Favorite Poems Old and New**, selected by Helen Ferris, read the excerpt from Lord Byron's "Childe Harold." What similarities do you see between Turner's paintings and Byron's poem? Would you agree with the art historians' comparison of the two? Why or why not?

- Look for "Burning of the Houses of Parliament" by Turner. How would you describe this painting? How is it different from a Neo-Classicist painting? Turner utilized great swirls of color on this painting. Would you consider it an effective use of color? Why or why not?

John Constable was the first major artist to paint in the open air, seeking to capture what was truly there rather than a "classicist" (stylized) rendering. His pictures seem to be almost a "snapshot" of the scene he painted.

- Find Constable's painting, "Hay Wain." This is among the most famous English landscape paintings ever accomplished, and one of the most reproduced for calendars! How would you describe the painting? How does it fit the description of the Romantic style? In **Favorite Poems Old and New**, selected by Helen Ferris, read the Wordsworth poem, "Written in March." What similarities do you see between Constable's portrayal of nature and this poem? Would you agree with the art historians' comparison of the two? Why or why not? How would you describe the differences between Turner and Constable? Which view of nature do you hold? Why?

Arts in Action

- Try your hand at creating a picture of the sea in the style of the Romantics. You may use colored pencils, watercolors, crayons, tempera, or oil paints. Use lots of color, a fluid style, light and shadow. Remember to make your outlines "fuzzy" rather than solid lines!

- Create a diorama of a pastoral landscape near your home, or an English landscape if you prefer, in the style of the Romantics. Rivers, hills, sheep, trees, flowers, clouds are all good choices to include. Experiment with "fuzzy" materials - like cotton balls for the clouds, wool for the sheep, moss for the grass, etc. - to create the look of the Romantics. Be creative!

"... OOPS!! ..."

Architecture

The Industrial Revolution brought about a revolution in architecture. Rather than architects designing only churches, palaces, and government structures, private industry now required the services of architects to design new buildings: factories, railroad stations, warehouses, and more.

In 1851, England astounded the world with its amazing technology and industry during the Great Exhibition (the first commercial and industrial World's Fair) in London. The exhibition was held in the Crystal Palace, a temporary greenhouse created of glass panels and iron framework. This structure covered nineteen acres and was tall enough to house the mighty elm trees standing in Hyde Park where the Crystal Palace was erected!

- Locate a photo of the Crystal Palace, designed by Joseph Paxton. What words would you use to describe this structure? Why was it fitting to hold the Great Exhibition in the Crystal Palace rather than in a "Neo-Classicist" style building?

Science

While staying in France in 1801, Robert Fulton invented the first submarine. Though he showed the invention to Napoleon, hoping to gain financing for this new machine, he found that Napoleon was not sufficiently impressed with its possibilities!

- In the book, **Make it Work! Ships**, a simple submarine is described which you can actually make! Learn the principles of how a submarine operates, the necessity for ballast, compressed air, and hydroplanes. Amazing!

James Watt was not the inventor of the steam engine, but his refinements are what it made it practical and useful. Since the first steam engines replaced the work done by horses, the strength of the engine is measured in "horsepower." Look up the equivalent in horses's power for one "horsepower."

- Discover what happens to water when it turns into steam. With adult supervision, place a pan filled three-quarters full of water on the stove. Cover the pan with a lid, and bring the water to a boil. Watch what happens to the lid. Does it move? The steam's action of pushing against the lid is what causes a steam engine to work. For more information on the workings of the steam engine, look it up in the encyclopedia!

- In **Make it Work! Machines**, an experiment is provided to show the power of the steam engine. You will actually build a model steam boat powered by a candle!

The uses of industrial power in spinning and weaving cloth brought about tremendous changes in Great Britain. Instead of families working together in their home to produce a small amount of fabric through spinning and weaving, mechanized factories were set up which greatly increased the output of material but also resulted in urbanization and slums.

- Try this: wind thread onto an empty bobbin (used in sewing machines) by hand, round and round. Time yourself to see how long it takes by hand. Next, with adult supervision, thread an empty bobbin using a sewing machine. Time how long this takes. Compare the time and the effort you expended to thread the bobbin. How does this correspond to the impact of the Industrial Revolution?

Samuel F.B. Morse

Music

The Romantic Period:

Emotional!

Expressive !

Innovative!

Poetry in musical form!

Idealizing nature! ***Larger than life!***

A time of contrasts:
large orchestras - solo pianos;   *instrumentals - vocals;*   *stormy - sensitive.*

The major composers of the Romantic time period are:

Rossini   *Mendelssohn*   *Berlioz*   *Schumann*
Chopin   *Donizetti*   *Liszt*   *Schubert*

Felix Mendelssohn brings us into the Romantic era through his use of "program music" - instrumental music which conveys an imaginative description of a scene or story. The concept of program music, then, was pursued by many composers in many parts of Europe throughout the 1800's.

- Listen to Mendelssohn's "A Midsummer Night's Dream" which is his delightful musical rendition of Shakespeare's play. As you listen, can you imagine the scenes which are being depicted through the music? Is this an effective means of expressing emotion? Can you explain the different ways that Mendelssohn used the orchestra to tell the story?

- Mendelssohn also created musical "landscapes" much as John Constable painted English landscapes. Listen to either the "Italian Symphony" or "Scotch Symphony" to hear how Mendelssohn can cause your imagination to see the scenes he is attempting to portray.

- For further study, listen to Berlioz's symphonies, or Chopin's technically demanding piano pieces.

Cooking

The study of Benito Juarez, Maximilian and the Mexican Empire made me hungry for Mexican food! Whether you serve this on Cinco de Mayo (the fifth of May) or not, it will always be a treat.

Chile con queso (Cheese Dip)

2 Tbsp. oil
1 cup chopped onions
2 garlic cloves, minced
1 4-oz. can chopped green chiles

1 8-oz. can stewed tomatoes, chopped
8 oz. Monterey Jack cheese, grated
8 oz. sharp Cheddar cheese, grated
1 cup sour cream

Heat oil in a large saucepan. Add onions and garlic, cooking until tender but not browned. Add chiles and tomatoes. Lower heat. Add cheese and cook until melted. Stir in sour cream. Cook until just heated - do not boil! Makes 4 cups of dip.

Serve with fried tortilla chips. One of our family favorites!

Idea Time

Creative Writing

- Giuseppe Garibaldi was a "larger than life" figure. Write his stirring biography for young children, telling the story of the fight for Italian independence. Illustrate it with pictures of his swashbuckling adventures!

- You are a freelance reporter. You smell a good story brewing when you learn about Robert Fulton's Nautilus submarine. Interview him after his disappointing visit with Napoleon. Will you submit your story to French newspapers or English newspapers? Write your story from the point of view you think you can sell.

- The Second Awakening began with a prayer meeting in New York City and went around the world. Write a narrative describing the unfolding events of this revival movement in the mid 1800's.

- Klemens von Metternich has hired you to "flush out revolutionaries." What got you this lucrative job is your proposal to place advertisements in newspapers throughout Europe which would lure revolutionaries out into the open. Your reputation is on the line - write the ad! (Remember, of course, that if the ad is too obvious, the censors will remove it.)

Art

- Draw a political cartoon of Commodore Perry going to Japan. Be sure to show the polite (though secretly outraged) countenances of the Japanese.

Drama

- Dramatize the life of Florence Nightingale. Include her privileged childhood, her struggle to go into nursing, and the Crimean War. Show her determination!

- Act out one or two of the miracles of God's provision in George Muller's orphanages. Remember that George made his needs known to God alone.

The Big Picture

- The Industrial Revolution had blessings and curses associated with it. Show your family, friends and/or neighbors what you would consider the best aspects of the Industrial Revolution, as well as the worst. Also, share what you have learned about the need for people to care for the poor, the sick, and the downtrodden. How can you apply this in your life, your church, your neighborhood, your nation?

Unit 3

The British Empire, The Intellectual Revolution, & The Missionaries of Africa

Queen Victoria

Unit Objectives:

- To understand the predominance of Queen Victoria's reign, and her family connection to the major monarchies of Europe;

- to study the practice of colonization by the European powers in the 1800's, and the results of colonization for good and for evil;

- to learn about Marxism, Darwinism, and the men who taught these theories to the world;

- to discover the amazing ministries and influence of Mary Slessor, David Livingstone, Andrew Murray, and others in Africa.

Meet the People & Study the Countries:

Here are some people you might meet in this unit:

In the Church:

David Livingstone   Mary Slessor   Andrew Murray
Samuel Morris

In the World:

Queen Victoria   Shaka   The Brothers Grimm
Karl Marx   Charles Darwin   Henry Stanley

You might wish to study one of these places in depth during this unit:

Africa   Australia/New Zealand

- **The Holy Bible**
  Deuteronomy 28:1-14; Psalm 3:3-6; Isaiah 52:7-10; Acts 8:26-39.

- **Queen Victoria** - World Leaders Past & Present, by Deirdre Shearman
  A well-balanced look at the longest-reigning queen in British history, this biography provides an excellent overview of the many facets of Queen Victoria, her family, her policies, and her reign. Highly recommended.   **Junior High & up**

- **Queen Victoria** - A World Landmark Book, by Noel Streatfeild
  This is an excellent "primer" for children concerning Queen Victoria's life. Learn about her isolation as a child, her governess, her accession to the throne at the age of nineteen, her prime ministers, Prince Albert, her children, and more. Highly recommended.
  Upper elem & up

- **Europe Around The World** - Cambridge Introduction to History, by Trevor Cairns
  This book is an excellent overview of the growth and development of European colonies around the world, and of how some of them achieved their independence. Focusing mostly on events in the 1800's, there are brief descriptions of the British Commonwealth, the South American countries, the development of Japan, the exploration of Siberia, and the scramble for Africa. Highly recommended!   **Upper elem & up**

- **Prophet of Revolution - Karl Marx** by Alfred Alpsler
  I was fascinated by this children's book on the life of Karl Marx. The story begins with Karl's father taking his children to the Lutheran church in Trier to be baptized, which would not seem unusual perhaps, unless one realizes that Karl's uncle was the Rabbi of Trier, as Karl's grandfather had been before him. To understand the growth and impact of communism, it is very helpful to understand the growth and impact of its founder - Karl Marx. Highly recommended.   **Upper elem & up**

- **Karl Marx** - Great Lives Series, by Nigel Hunter
This is a much shorter biography than the one listed above. It contains all of the essential information about Marx's life and work, though it does not show the inconsistencies of Marxism or of his lifestyle.   **Upper elem & up**

- **Darwin on Trial** by Phillip E. Johnson
This is one of the definitive books explaining the "faith" factor necessary for Darwinist evolution - faith in naturalism. Highly recommended!   **High School & up**

- **Understanding The Times** by David Noebel
Read especially the chapter about secular humanist biology and Darwinism. It is excellent!   **Junior High & up**

- **Seven Men Who Rule the World from the Grave** by Dave Breese
Darwin, Marx, Freud, Kierkegaard are some of the people profiled in this thought-provoking book. Mr. Breese has done us an invaluable service by showing how the philosophies of these men have dramatically impacted both our world and the Church. Highly recommended!
                                                                                                                       High School & up

- **Exploration of Africa** - A Horizon Caravel Book, by Thomas Sterling
The exploration of the "Dark Continent" took place almost entirely during the 1800's. This excellent book introduces us to the most important explorers of Africa, including Mungo Park, David Livingstone, and Henry Stanley. We also learn of the various river systems, the mysterious cities (like Timbuctoo), and the slave trade conducted in Africa. It is important to remember that countries desperately needed this information in order to set up their African colonies, but that missionary societies were able to benefit as well. Very informative!
                                                                                                                       Upper elem & up

- **Shaka - King of the Zulus** by Diane Stanley and Peter Venema
A children's biography of a military genius, this is the story of the Zulu who united his people and turned them into the finest warrior nation in Africa.   **Mid elem & up**

- **Escape from the Slave Traders** - Trailblazer Books, by Dave & Neta Jackson
Historical fiction for children, this title describes the work of David Livingstone to eradicate the slave trade in Africa. Highly recommended!   **Mid elem & up**

- **David Livingstone** - Christian Heroes Then and Now, by Janet & Geoff Benge
Wonderfully written, this series of Christian biographies is fascinating, factual, and historically accurate. Meet David Livingstone, whose travels through Africa opened up the Dark Continent. His concern was twofold: that the Gospel would be preached and that slavery would be ended. Highly recommended!   **Upper elem & up**

- **The Paradox of David Livingstone** - Christian History, Issue 56 (Vol. XVI, No. 4)
This edition of Christian History is dedicated entirely to the life and impact of David Livingstone. Did you know that Livingstone worked 14-hour days in a cotton factory when he was ten years old? He was the first European to see several of Africa's scenic wonders. Highly recommended!   **Upper elem & up**

- **David Livingstone** by Jeanette Eaton
  An excellent biography of Livingstone for children!   **Mid elem & up**

- **Stanley And Livingstone - Expeditions Through Africa** by Clint Twist
  This is worth searching for! It is filled with pictures and brief descriptions of the famous
  African explorers. It includes brief overviews of the people of Africa, the Scramble for Africa,
  and independence. Highly recommended!   **Mid elem & up**

- **Henry Stanley and David Livingstone** - World's Great Explorers Series, by Susan Clinton
  In this volume you will find a thorough yet readable description of the lives of these two men
  and of the results of their meeting. Fascinating!   **Mid elem & up**

- **Trial by Poison** - Trailblazer Books, by Dave & Neta Jackson
  Historical fiction for children, this is the story of Mary Slessor and her ministry in West Africa.
  Highly recommended!   **Mid elem & up**

- **Mary Slessor** - Christian Heroes Then and Now, by Janet & Geoff Benge
  Wonderfully written, this series of Christian biographies is fascinating, factual, and historically
  accurate. Mary Slessor was an amazing missionary who desired to live simply among the
  unreached people of Calabar (known as Nigeria today). Learn more about her life and
  ministry in this excellent book. Highly recommended!   **Upper elem & up**

- **Mary Slessor: Heroine of Calabar** - Women of Faith Series, by Basil Miller
  Mary Slessor had such an impact on the people she ministered to that she was known as the
  "Mother of Calabar." She was also the first woman in the British Empire to be appointed vice
  consul. Singularly important.   **Upper elem & up**

- **Samuel Morris** - Men of Faith Series, by Lindley Baldwin
  Subtitled, "the African boy God sent to prepare an American University for its mission to the
  world," this book tells the incredible story of a young man who miraculously escaped from a
  torturous death in Liberia and eventually came to America in the 1880's. Amazing!
                  Upper elem & up

- **Andrew Murray** - Men of Faith Series, by Dr. William Lindner, Jr.
  Born in South Africa, Andrew Murray was used mightily by God in a revival that took place in
  his country in 1860. Many have been blessed and challenged by his devotionals, but the story
  of his life, set into its historical moment, is incredible! Highly recommended!
                  Upper elem & up

- **South Africa** - Enchantment of the World Series, by R. Conrad Stein
  This series of books gives a brief overview of the country's history, its geography, and culture.
  An excellent "primer" for discovering more about South Africa and the South African people.
  Learn more about the struggle between the British and the Boers, the Zulu kingdom, and the
  impact of apartheid. Highly recommended!   **Upper elem & up**

- **The Story of Australia** - A World Landmark Book, by A. Grove Day
Beginning in 1787, England sent her overflow of convicts to an unsettled land with relatively few native people - Australia. This excellent children's book tells the story of the development of this country.   My favorite anecdote has to do with Caroline Chisolm - the "Moses" of Australia. Highly recommended!   **Upper elem & up**

- **Maori and Settler** by G.A. Henty
Following Henty's fashion for very factual presentation of his fiction, this is a fascinating history of New Zealand, telling the story of the troubles between British settlers and a few tribes of the Maori. I was interested to learn that prior to this time, the Maoris had eagerly accepted Christianity! Highly recommended!   **Upper elem & up**

- **The British Empire and Commonwealth of Nations** by Douglas Liversidge
The story told in this fascinating book is of the British Empire becoming the Commonwealth of Nations. Learn how the Commonwealth works, what it means (and does not mean!), and what countries are part of it.   **Junior High & up**

- **The British Raj and Indian Nationalism** by Malcom Yapp
India and England have been connected for centuries. This book describes both the beneficial as well as the detrimental aspects of the British Empire in India.   **Upper elem & up**

- **Jane Eyre** by Charlotte Bronte
Classic literature set in Victorian England, this is one of the most celebrated romances of all time - because of the integrity of the heroine.   **High School & up**

- **Dates with Destiny - The 100 Most Important Dates in Church History**
by A. Kenneth Curtis, J. Stephen Lang, and Randy Petersen
Beginning with the year 64 in Rome and continuing to 1976, this book is filled with short descriptions of events and people within the Church. For this chapter read about David Livingstone and Kierkegaard. Highly recommended!   **Upper elem & up**

- **From Jerusalem to Irian Jaya - A Biographical History of Christian Missions**
by Ruth A. Tucker
This is the best book on the history of world missions available. Included are short biographies of missionaries all over the world, categorized by their geographical area of service.   I consider this an indispensable resource for the study of **World Empires, World Missions, World Wars**. For this chapter, read pages 139 - 164. Highly recommended!
Upper elem & up

- **Building the Suez Canal** - A Horizon Caravel Book, by S.C. Burchell
What a fascinating story! Learn about Ferdinand de Lessep, the man who built the canal against tremendous odds. This book gives the reader a tremendous sense of what was involved - both politically and structurally - to get the job accomplished. Highly recommended!   **Upper elem & up**

- **Michael Faraday: Father of Electronics** by Charles Ludwig
  A well-written story, this is a wonderful biography of the Englishman who was a devout Christian and a remarkable scientist. He invented the electric generator and the transformer, as well as building an electric motor - one of the first! Highly recommended!

  Mid elem & up

- **Once Upon A Time! - A story of the Brothers Grimm** by Robert Quackenbush
  This is an absolutely delightful book about the two brothers who, through their thorough-going research, brought many of the world's best fairy tales to light from their almost forgotten past. The Brothers Grimm lived in a German kingdom that was conquered by Napoleon, eventually ending up in Berlin at the invitation of the King of Prussia! Highly recommended!

  Great Read Aloud

- **Video: Zulu Dawn**
  This movie shows the battle at Isandlwana (Zululand) between the British and Zulu in 1879. The heavily armed and sophisticated British soldiers were completely overwhelmed and defeated during this battle.

  Junior High & up

Talk Together

Sebastopol harbor

- Listen to **What in the World's Going On Here?, Volume Two**, Tape Two - Side One. What were the most interesting aspects to you of the Victorian Era and colonization? Why? What other questions about this time period would you like to have answered?
  History Journal: Write those questions down and, as you study more material, write the answers to your questions. Also, write short bios of the people you study whom you find interesting. Illustrate the bios.

- Why do you think countries wanted their monarchs to be from a royal family, regardless of what nationality the royals were? Do you think this made a difference in European politics? Why or why not?

- What do you think it would be like to have your cousin be the reigning monarch of a country that was at war with your own country? Do you think that Queen Victoria's grandchildren had problems with this issue? Why or why not?

- Why do you think William Wilberforce's book, "**A Practical View of the Prevailing Religious System**," was so popular in England? What impact do you think it might have had on the people of England and on their activities?

- In the 1800's, European countries looked upon the acquisition of colonies as necessary and good. What do you think the reasons were for believing this? Do you think there were any positive results that came from colonization? If so, what were they? Do you think there were any negative results that came from colonization? If so, what were they?

- What did the colonies provide to their mother country? What did the mother country provide to the colonies? Do you think this was a mutually beneficial relationship? Why or why not?

- What do you think would have been the effect of the European countries NOT having access to the raw materials found in the colonies? What might this have done to the Industrial Revolution?

- Why do you think the British colonies wanted independence? In your opinion, how would this new independence have effected the former colonies? Why do you think that many of Britain's former colonies chose to stay connected to Great Britain in the British Commonwealth?

- Why do you think the European powers divided up Africa without concern for tribal boundaries? Do you think the Europeans assumed the Africans would react to these boundaries as the smaller European countries had done when they were divided up among the larger European powers? In which African nations did this prove to be an accurate expectation? What effect do you think the exploration of Africa had upon this "scramble" for European colonies?

- Who were the major explorers of Africa? Where were they from? What other impact did these explorers have upon the people of Africa or of Europe?

- Why do you think the slave trade was so significant in Africa? (Consider the economics.) David Livingstone believed that commerce and Christianity would help to eradicate the slave trade of Africa. What were some of the changes he expected would come through commerce and Christianity?

- Do you think it was difficult for Henry Stanley to find Livingstone? Imagine you were with Stanley's group. What do you think it would have been like following someone who didn't know where to look for the person he was searching for? Do you suppose Livingstone was surprised to see Stanley? Why or why not? What effect do you think Livingstone had on Stanley? Why?

- Do you think it was unusual for a woman to do what Mary Slessor did - live by herself in the jungle among the native people? Why or why not? Why do you think she wanted to do that? Why do you suppose the British government made her their first female magistrate in the British Empire?

- Do you think that the nature of an absolute monarchy in Prussia and the policies of Klemens von Metternich effected Karl Marx's ideas when he was a student? Why or why not? Why do you suppose Marx was allowed to settle in England after having been driven out of some of the European countries? Do you think he was considered effective by the people of his time? Why or why not?

- Charles Darwin was the grandson of a famous scientist - Erasmus Darwin - who had already been considering the idea of evolution. Do you suppose there was a correlation between Darwin's early pondering of these ideas of evolution and the "evidence" that he found on his travels aboard the HMS Beagle? Is it possible to interpret what we see based upon what we want to believe? Do you know examples of that? How do you think a scientist who believed the Bible to be true would have interpreted the evidence Darwin encountered on that voyage?

- What importance is given to Darwin's theory? Do you think its impact has extended to more than the scientific community? How might people utilize this concept? For instance, what did Karl Marx think of Darwin's theory?

- Why do you suppose philosophies like "God is dead" (Nietzsche) gained a following? Do you see any correlation between this and Darwin's theories? Explain what the correlation might be.

David Livingston

Teaching Time!

Seminar Outline

I. Victorian Era
  - A. Queen Victoria
    1. Reigned from 1837 to 1901 - the longest reign in history!
    2. Her family background and connections - German Saxe Coburgs
       - a. Leopold
         1. Marries daughter of English king
         2. She dies in childbirth
         3. He becomes King of Belgium
       - b. his sister marries the Duke of Kent
         1. she gives birth to a baby girl - Victoria
       - c. Victoria marries Prince Albert (her cousin)
       - d. A cousin marries Queen of Portugal
       - e. Another cousin becomes Duke of Wurtemberg
       - f. Victoria's daughter marries crown prince of Prussia
       - g. Victoria's grandson becomes Kaiser Bill (of WWI) (1859-1941)
       - h. Victoria's eldest son was Edward VII, King of England
       - i. Victoria's daughter, Alice, married Duke of Hess
         1. Their daughter marries Nicholas II of Russia
         2. Killed during the Bolshevik (or October) revolution
  - B. Revivals and Reform
    1. William Wilberforce's "A Practical View of the Prevailing Religious System of Professed Christians in the Higher and Middle Classes in the Country contrasted with Real Christianity."
       - a. 7,500 copies sold in first six months
       - b. Very influential in middle and upper classes
    2. True Christianity contrasted to an empty form
  - C. Family Life
    1. Queen Victoria and Prince Albert had nine children
    2. Their love of family and home influenced the nation

II. British Empire
  - A. During Queen Victoria's reign
    1. Covered 1/4 of the world's land and 1/4 of the world's population
    2. "The sun never sets on the British Empire."
  - B. Colonies in Caribbean, Africa, Asia, Australia, and Pacific
  - C. Ruled from London - united under Queen
  - D. Why the Empire worked so well
    1. Raw materials for manufacturing
    2. A market for manufactured goods from the mother country
    3. Agent in every port, every island
       - a. Organized local products to be exported
       - b. Created markets for British imports

E. Colonies gain their independence
    1. Home Rule to Canada in 1867
    2. Independence to Australia - 1901
    3. Independence to India - 1947
    4. Dominion Status

III. Colonization by other European Countries
    A. Belgium took Congo - Belgian Congo - Zaire
    B. France
        1.West and North Africa (Morocco, Algeria)
        2. Asia (Indochina - Vietnam)
        3. Caribbean
    C. Germany
        1. German East Africa
        2. SW Africa
    D. Italians took Libya
    E. Holland
        1. South Africa (Boers)
        2. Philippines
    F. Portugal
        1. Brazil
        2. Angola
        3. Mozambique
    G. Spain
        1. South America
        2. Central America
        3. Spanish Morocco

IV. Scramble for Africa
    A. Rival European countries seeking African colonies
        1. Formal process in 1884
        2. Cut up Africa like a cake
    B. Traditional African boundaries ignored completely

V. Missionaries in Africa
    A. David Livingstone - 1813 - 1873
        1. Sent by London Missionary Society in 1840 to S. Africa
        2. Married Robert Moffat's daughter
        3. In 1852 sent wife and children back to England
        4. Made a four year, 6,000 mile journey
            a. Coast to coast
            b. Angola on the Atlantic to Mozambique on the Indian Ocean
        5. "I will place no value on anything I have... except in relation to Kingdom of Christ."
        6. Went back to England with his discoveries
        7. Back to Africa, was not heard from for years...
        8. Henry Stanley found him

9. African customs, geography and slave trade described by Livingstone

    B. Mary Slessor (1848 - 1915)

        1. Sent to Calabar (W Africa) - 1876

            a. Warring tribes in Calabar - fierce, violent, drunken

            b. Twins killed at birth, mothers driven away

        2. Won the chiefs over by fearlessness and dedication, medical and linguistic skills, and sense of humor

        3. Became known as Ma Slessor, "Mother of Calabar"

        4. Appointed the first woman magistrate in British Empire!

VI. Intellectual Revolution - Marxism, Darwinism, and Heresy in the Church

    A. Karl Marx (1818 - 1883)

        1. Born in Prussia (like George Muller)

        2. Studied philosophy at U of Berlin 1836

        3. Could not get teaching job due to his opposition to government

        4. Published **Communist Manifesto** - 1848

        5. Exiled to England

        6. **Das Kapital**, his major work - 1867

    B. Charles Darwin (1809 -1882)

        1. Grandson of a famous scientist (Erasmus Darwin)

        2. Aboard HMS Beagle - 1831-1836

        3. Publishes his diary - "evidence"

        4. **"On the Origin of the Species by Means of Natural Selection"** - 1859

        5. Marx - justified "struggle for power among social classes"

    C. New humanistic philosophies in the Church

        1. Nietzsche (1844-1900)

            a. Prussian Theologian who said "God is Dead"

        2. Hegel

        3. Kierkegaard

    D. Cults

        1. Christian Science

        2. Mormonism

        3. Theosophy (seances, etc.)

Timeline

On your timeline, mark Queen Victoria; home rule in Canada; independence for Australia, New Zealand, India; the Scramble for Africa; David Livingstone; Mary Slessor; Karl Marx; Charles Darwin; Nietzsche.

Research & Reporting

- Find one of the books listed at the beginning of this unit, along with the encyclopedia or other history resource book, for basic information on Queen Victoria and the Victorian Era, or the British Empire. Write a report on what you learn about this time period.

- Make a chart showing Queen Victoria's parents, her uncle Leopold, children and grandchildren. Show the country of residence, the alliances of that country, who was the reigning monarch of that country, and the years that any of her relatives were in power.

- Research and report on the Crystal Palace Exhibition - the brain child of Prince Albert. What was the purpose? Who was the exhibition for? What was on exhibit? When was it built? How long did it last? What countries were represented? What effect did this have on England? - On Prince Albert? - On Queen Victoria?

- Research and report on the British colonies during the second half of the nineteenth centuries. You may choose to focus on one colony, or compare and contrast the various colonies around the world. Analyze the positive effect of colonization for the colonies; for Great Britain. Compare and contrast this with the negative effect of colonization on the colonies and on Great Britain.

- Research and report on the issues of trade with the colonies. Describe the economics of colonial trade ("follow da money"); imports and exports; the necessary vessels used in the transportation of trade goods; the importance of safe trade routes; the opportunities for missionaries to travel around the world via the trade vessels. Were there any colonies which had their own factories? Were any colonies benefited after independence by the trade established with Great Britain?

- Compare and contrast the independence of the U.S. (a former British colony) with the Commonwealth status of Canada, Australia, or New Zealand. Examine the ways each of these former colonies established their own form of independence.

- Research and report on the British colonization of Australia and New Zealand. What was the reason for settlement in Australia? - In New Zealand? How were the native people treated in Australia? - In New Zealand? What did the colonists use for trade with the mother country?

- Research and report on the colonization of the Congo (Zaire) by Belgium. Why was this an attractive land to King Leopold II? What was the effect of colonization on the Africans in the Congo area? Examine the current political situation, then compare and contrast it with the colonial period.

- Research and report on one of the French colonies - in Africa, Asia or the Caribbean. What kinds of raw materials did France utilize from its colonies? What did France export back to its colonies? Describe colonization under the French government. Study and describe what happened to these colonies after independence from France.

- Research and report on Germany's colonies in Africa. What kinds of raw materials did Germany utilize from its colonies? What benefits did the Germans provide for their colonies? In what ways was Germany benefited by its colonies? Study and describe what happened to these colonies after independence from Germany.

- Research and report on Italy's colonization of Libya. What was the effect of this colonization on Libya? - On Italy? What happened to Libya after its independence from Italy?

- Dutch settlers were the original European settlers in South Africa. Eventually, however, the British began colonizing the area. Research and report on the Great Trek of the Boers (Dutch settlers), the relationship between the British and the Boers, and the Boer War. Be sure to consider the Zulu nation and their effect upon the Boers and the British.

- Research and report on Holland's colonization of the Philippines. What was the effect of colonization upon the Philippinos? - Upon the Dutch? What happened to the Philippines after its independence from Holland? Why and how did the U.S. become involved in the Philippines? Describe the history of this relationship.

- Research and report on one of the Portuguese colonies in Africa or in South America. What kinds of raw materials did Portugal utilize from its colonies? What did Portugal export back to its colonies? Describe colonization under the Portuguese. Study and describe what happened to these colonies after independence from Portugal.

- Study and write about Spain's colonies in the New World or in Morocco. What was the most profitable resource for Spain in the New World? What other goods were exported to Spain? What did Spain provide for its colonies? How were these colonies ruled? What effect did colonization have upon the colonies? - Upon Spain? What brought about their independence? How have these former colonies fared since independence?

- Research and report on the Scramble for Africa in the 1880's. Which European countries and leaders were involved? How much of Africa was at stake? Make a chart showing how this effected the boundaries of Africa. Which of the European countries controlled which of the African territories? What were the natural resources and riverways in each of these areas?

- What difficulties did the European nations encounter in controlling, governing, and managing these colonies?

- Research and report on the life and ministry of David Livingstone. What were his strengths? What were his weaknesses? Describe his childhood, his family life, his relationship to Africans. Evaluate his success as a missionary and as an explorer.

- Research and report on the life and ministry of Mary Slessor. Describe her childhood and her first years in Africa. What changes did she make when she returned to Africa? What evils did she combat in the culture of the people of Calabar? How successful was she? Describe her later years. What were the responsibilities of a magistrate in the British Empire? What qualified her for this position?

- Andrew Murray was one of the most profound Christian devotional writers of history. Research and report on his life and ministry in South Africa. How did his views on prayer, child-rearing, and Christianity change the lives of believers? Describe his own family relationships and walk with God.

- Research and report on Karl Marx and his philosophy of communism. Describe his childhood in Prussia, his university days, his years of exile. What was the purpose of the **Communist Manifesto** of 1848? Who was Engels? What was the purpose of **Das Kapital** (1867)? What did he leave for Engels to do? How did he support his family? What was the impact of his writings?

- What is the continuing impact of Marx's writings? What is the nature and intent of Marx's philosophy?

- Make a chart of the nations of Marxism. Show all the countries that have been under Marxist systems, that are still under Marxist systems, and that are being pursued by Marxist people.

- Study and write about Charles Darwin. What had he studied prior to his voyage on the HMS Beagle? What did he observe on his voyage? How did he interpret his observations? What was the respone to his publications?

- List or chart the points of Darwinism which attempt to explain the origin of life. Chart the contrasting points of Biblical science which explain the origin of life.

Brain Stretchers

- Study and report on William Wilberforce's book, "A Practical View of the Prevailing Religious System of Professed Christians in the Higher and Middle Classes in the Country contrasted with Real Christianity." What were the conditions of the Church at this point in English history? What subjects did Wilberforce address in this book? What was the impact upon the people of England? Compare and contrast the social class being addressed by this book with the group of people promoting slavery contrary to Wilberforce. Evaluate whether he was dealing with the same group of people.

- Study and write about the Battle of Isandhlwana in 1879 between the Zulu kingdom and the British in Zululand. Why was this battle fought? What was the outcome? How did that effect British morale and policy? Describe the battle tactics of the Zulu. How effective were these tactics? Why is this battle historically important?

- Compare and contrast each of the European colonies in Africa with the African country today. What systems did the European powers put in place that still exist (politics, economics, trade, technology, education, etc.)? Evaluate which of the African countries today are the most stable. Is there a correlation between their stability and what form of government their former colonial masters used?

- Read Francis Schaeffer's book, **How Should We Then Live**, concerning Nietzsche, Hegel and Kierkegaard. How did their views differ from earlier humanistic philosophers? How did their philosophies effect the world?

Vocabulary

colonization	Marxism	Darwinism	accession	scramble
naturalism	apartheid	trekking	caravan	jungle
penal colony	grassland	scrubland	commerce	malaria

Many of the terms in this unit focus on Africa and exploration.

- Find as many African terms as you can and define them.

Hands On!

**Maps
and
Mapping**

- Using an atlas, encyclopedia, or other resource locate the former colonies of Great Britain - such as Australia, New Zealand, India, Canada, South Africa. Also locate the Galapagos Islands, Nigeria (formerly Calabar), Isandhlwana, Victoria Falls, the Zambezi River, and the headwaters of the Nile.

- What are the names of the cities and countries that today occupy the same area? What is the capital city, religion, population, major export, and type of government in each modern country? What is the status of Christianity in these countries?

- On a clean worksheet map, draw lines tracing the journeys of David Livingston and show Mary Slessor's place of ministry. Also show the route settlers took to settle Australia, New Zealand, India and/or South Africa.

- Consult a relief map to discover the terrain found in the areas in Africa where the early missionaries worked. Also, discover the terrain in Australia and New Zealand. Are there deserts, forest, mountains, islands? Label them. What kind of climate is typical in each of the different terrains? How did these different terrains and climates affect the missionaries' or explorers' ability to travel through Africa? How did these different terrains and climates affect the British settlers who colonized Australia and New Zealand?

Reception of the Chief

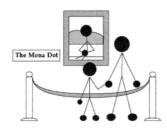

The Mona Dot

Art Appreciation

During the mid-1800's in France, a new style of landscape painting began - called the "Barbizon school" - which followed in the footsteps of John Constable and Joseph Turner. The most noted painter of this style was Jean-François Millet. However, he seldom painted pure landscapes, choosing instead to focus on peasants at their tasks, with the landscape in the background.

It is interesting that Millet's first successful paintings of peasants date from the Year of Revolutions - 1848. Though he denied any political or socialist message in his paintings, yet his focus on workers was certainly timely. He wrote, "peasant subjects suit my temperament best; for I must confess, even if you think me a socialist, that the human side of art is what touches me most."

- Locate a picture of Millet's "The Gleaners." Would you describe this painting as realistic? Why or why not? How would you describe the women who are gleaning? Do you think Millet esteemed their work and worth? Why or why not? This painting is considered by many art historians to be one of the great classic masterpieces of French art. Would you agree? Compare Millet with Turner and Constable. How are they similar? How are they different? If you could own a painting from one of these artists, which one would you choose? Why?

- Locate a picture of Millet's "The Angelus." What are the couple doing? Is this painting realistic? Why or why not? "The Angelus" was Millet's most popular painting. Why do you think it was so popular? 1 Thessalonians 4:11 tells us "that you also aspire to lead a quiet life, to mind your own business, and to work with your own hands, as we commanded you..." How does Millet's painting illustrate this scripture?

Arts in Action

- Look at Millet's "The Gleaners." Do you notice the people working in the background? Did Millet paint them the same size as the women who are gleaning? Why not? Try this: Sketch a picture of someone working. Add people and a setting in the background (like a park, house, or field). Remember to make the items in the background smaller than the items in the foreground.

- Create an album of your family! Show your family members in day-to-day life with photos or drawings that are simple, "quiet," industrious, and pious to create an album that reflects Millet's art. It may be more "Millet-esque" if you can use black and white photos. You may be able to use old photos from your grandparents. Be sure to title each photo or drawing - following the style of Millet. Have fun!

"... OOPS!! ..."

Architecture

In 1839, the Gothic Revival in England became the pronounced style of architecture with the commencement of the building of Parliament at Westminster. The Gothic Revival had a powerful champion in John Ruskin, an art critic of the nineteenth century, who believed classical architecture was pagan and immoral, declaring Gothic to be the only true Christian architecture. During this time, the Tractarian revival, also known as "the Oxford movement," arose in the "High" Church of England. The Tractarian revival - a reaction against the possibility of the disestablishment of the Anglican Church in England - was expressed architecturally through Gothic Revival.

- Locate a photo of the Houses of Parliament in London, England. Designed by Sir Charles Barry and A.W. Pugin, this is an excellent example of Gothic Revival architecture. How does it differ from a Neo-Classical style building? How does it differ from the Crystal Palace? The Royal Throne inside the House of Lords was designed by A.W. Pugin. Locate a picture of it, determine what former century or era it looks like, and then consider that it was built between 1844 and 1852!

- All Saints Church, Margaret Street, in London was designed by William Butterfield. Find a picture of the interior of All Saints. Would you describe this style as Gothic? Why or why not? How does it differ from neo-classical?

Science

Michael Faraday was one of the greatest physicists of history. His work on electricity and magnetism paved the way for the everyday usage of electricity. He was also a devout Christian and a humble man.

Mr. Faraday was the first one to discover that magnetism can produce electricity. Here is a simple experiment to show his discovery:

- You will need a piece of electrical wire about two yards long, a bar magnet, and a small compass. Peel one inch of covering off both ends of the wire. Loosely wrap one end of the wire around your hand about ten times to form a coil. Slip the wire off your hand leaving it coiled. Wrap the other end of the wire around the compass about five times, leaving the wire on the compass. Now twist the two peeled ends of the wire together. Move the bar magnet in and out of the empty coils while watching what happens to the compass. Did the needle move? The compass demonstrates that there is a small electrical current being produced. What happens when you leave the bar magnet inside of the coils? Outside of the coils? Move the bar magnet in and out several times again, using different speeds. What happens now?

- For more fantastic science experiments with electricity, look for books in your library. For materials for science experiments, we also suggest contacting:
  Home Training Tools, 2827 Buffalo Horn Drive, Laurel, MT 59044, (800) 860-6272

Music

Nationalistic Music:
      Ethnic themes
            Ethnic melodies and harmonies

The major composers of Nationalistic music are:
Wagner   Tchaikovsky   Smetana   Rimsky-Korsakov

Peter I. Tchaikovsky, the great Russian composer, exemplifies nationalism in music by his use of Russian sounding melodies, typical Russian harmonies and important Russian stories for use in his musical masterpieces. One of his best known compositions is the "1812 Overture" which musically tells the story of Napoleon's defeat in Russia.

- Listen to the "1812 Overture." Can you follow the scenes of battle as it progresses from the arrogant French invasion to the brutal approach of the Russian winter to the tumultuous victory of the Russian people? Do you hear any melodies repeated throughout this music? Hum the melodies for your family - and then tell them the story of Napoleon's defeat!

- For further study in this time period, listen to the operas of Giuseppi Verdi (especially **Aida**) and Georges Bizet (**Carmen**).

Cooking

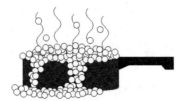

The missionaries to Africa had the opportunity to try many new dishes (it is part of the job description!). Here is a taste of South Africa for you to try.

Bobotee - Meat Timbales from South Africa

2 Tbsp. butter
1 onion, chopped
1 clove garlic, minced
1 slice bread
1 cup milk
2 eggs, beaten
1 pound ground beef
1 Tbsp. curry powder

Juice of one lemon
1/4 cup chopped almonds
8 dried apricots, soaked and chopped
1/4 cup raisins
1/4 cup chutney
Salt
Pepper

Preheat oven to 350 degrees. Melt the butter in a pan, sauté the onion and garlic until tender and just beginning to brown. Soak the bread in the milk, then squeeze dry. Beat the eggs into the remaining milk. Combine the meat, bread and onions with the remaining ingredients. Stir in half the egg-milk mixture. Place the mixture in a greased baking dish. Top with remaining egg mixture and bake until the custard sets, about 45 minutes. Serve with plain rice. Serves 6.

Idea Time

Creative Writing

- You have been asked to interview Mary Slessor after her appointment as vice-consul - the first woman in the British Empire to receive this appointment! However, before you can interview her, you have to find her in the jungles of Calabar. Write a letter home to your parents describing your adventures through the jungle and your interview with the "Mother of Calabar."

- You just recently arrived as a settler in New Zealand. Write a letter to friends back home in England to try to inspire them to come join you. Be sure to include details of what the islands of New Zealand are like, the climate, the perfect growing conditions, the native people, the other settlers, etc.

- Karl Marx has been coming daily to the British library in London for years. As a librarian, you try to learn more about your patrons so as to better serve their needs. However, when you read about Marx's philosophy, you are horrified. Write a letter to the editor of the London Times expressing your outrage over someone using the resources of the library to try to pull down your government - that same government who funds the library!

- Write a children's version of the life of Queen Victoria. Be sure to include descriptions of her children's and grandchildren's royal lives.

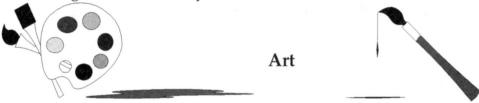

Art

- Draw a political cartoon showing the "Scramble for Africa." Be sure to show the eagerness of the European governments and the surprise of the African people.

- Draw a political cartoon of Darwin's trip to the Galapagos Islands. Show his grandfather's influence on Darwin's theory of evolution.

Drama

- Dramatize the meeting of David Livingstone and Henry Stanley in Africa. Remember, Stanley did not know where Livingstone was when he began his search!

The Big Picture

- In this unit we have studied people who have brought great blessing to the world and people who have brought great cursing. Put together a demonstration, using the people and events from this unit, showing the principle that "ideas have consequences." Share it with family, friends, and/or neighbors.

Unit Four

Franco-Prussian War, The Salvation Army & The China Inland Mission

William I

Unit Objectives:

- To understand the rise of Prussian nationalism under von Bismarck, and the impact of the Franco-Prussian War of 1870 on France and Germany;

- to learn about the beginnings of the Salvation Army and how it ministered to the needs of the urban poor in England;

- to study Hudson Taylor and the China Inland Mission and how God used them to bring the Gospel to China's billions;

- to discover the work of Amy Carmichael and John Hyde in India;

- to read about the Student Volunteer Movement and D.L. Moody.

Meet the People & Study the Countries:

Here are some people you might meet in this unit:

In the Church:

Hudson Taylor	Charles Spurgeon	William & Catherine Booth
D. L. Moody	Fanny Crosby	Amy Carmichael
John Hyde	John Paton	

In the World:

Otto von Bismarck	Napoleon III	Louis Pasteur
Alexander Graham Bell	Theodore Roosevelt	Kaiser Wilhelm I
Thomas Alva Edison		

You might wish to study one of these places in depth during this unit:

Prussia	The German Empire	China (also Unit 9)
South Pacific Islands		

- **The Holy Bible**
Proverbs 11:24-25, 14:31; Micah 6:8; Jonah 3:2-3

- **Otto von Bismarck** - World Leaders Past & Present, by Jonathan E. Rose
This is the man who, in his first speech to the Prussian parliament, announced, "the great questions of the day will be decided not by speeches and majority votes... but by blood and iron." His governing policy, realpolitik, meant that "any alliance could be broken, any program abandoned, any supporter betrayed in the ultimate struggle for power." Read more about his influence in world affairs in this excellent biography. Highly recommended.
                                                                                Junior High & up

- **Democratic Despot** by T.B. Corley
This is a compelling, in-depth biography of Napoleon III, nephew of Napoleon Bonaparte and Emperor of the Second Empire of France. Through Napoleon III's maneuverings, the Crimean War was fought and won by the French and English; Mexico briefly had a Hapsburg emperor - Maximillian; the French navy began to rival the British navy; and the Prussians were able to form the Second German Empire after their defeat of Napoleon III's troops in the Franco-Prussian War of 1870.   **High School & up**

- **Linnea in Monet's Garden** by Christina Bjork, Illustrated by Lena Anderson
This is a delightful book to use for introducing children to the paintings of Monet. This is one to own!   **Elementary & up**

- **Vincent van Gogh** - Why They Became Famous,
by Sergio Bitossi, English adaption by Vincent Buranelli
One of the most important painters of the 1800's, Vincent van Gogh was nonetheless one of the most tormented men of his age. This biography provides fascinating glimpses into his childhood, his career, his search for meaning (including his attempts to preach the Gospel to poor miners!).   **Mid elem & up**

- **Louis Pasteur** by Laura N. Wood
  A fascinating biography of one of the greatest scientists of all time. He discovered a cure for rabies, disproved spontaneous generation, developed vaccines, and gave us "pasteurization." Excellent!   **Upper elem & up**

- **The Life of Louis Pasteur** - Pioneers in Health and Medicine, by Marcia Newfield
  This is a wonderful biography of Louis Pasteur, is filled with brief anecdotes about his life and his work. Highly recommended!   **Mid elem & up**

- **Kidnapped by River Rats** - Trailblazer Books, by Dave & Neta Jackson
  Historical fiction for children, this title describes the ministry of William and Catherine Booth, the founders of the Salvation Army. Highly recommended!   **Mid elem & up**

- **William Booth** - Men of Faith Series, by David Bennett
  Subtitled, "The passionate founder of the Salvation Army who championed the cause of the poor," this biography tells the incredible story of a man who ministered to people in the midst of their hopelessness. Highly recommended!   **Junior High & up**

- **D. L. Moody** - Men of Faith Series, by David Bennett
  Subtitled "The unconventional American evangelist who reached 100 million people with the gospel," this is the story of a man whose ministry profoundly touched both the British Isles and the United States. Flowing out of this ministry were many who ended up on the mission fields of the world.   **Upper elem & up**

- **Hudson Taylor** - Christian Heroes Then and Now, by Janet & Geoff Benge
  Wonderfully written, this series of Christian biographies is fascinating, factual, and historically accurate. Hudson Taylor went to China as a missionary in 1854. His story is one of my personal favorites in all of Christendom. Highly recommended!   **Mid elem & up**

- **Hudson Taylor** - Men of Faith Series, by J. Hudson Taylor
  Hudson Taylor's autobiography, this is filled with the goodness of God in the midst of the difficulties of his life. It tells the story of Taylor's life until 1866, and the beginning of the China Inland Mission. Highly recommended!   **Upper elem & up**

- **Hudson Taylor's Spiritual Secret** by Dr. and Mrs. Howard Taylor
  This book changed my life. It not only tells the story of Hudson Taylor's life, but also shows how he learned to rest in God's abilities, not his own. Highly recommended!
                                                                                          Junior High & up

- **China: A History to 1949** - Enchantment of the World Series, by Valjean McLenighan
  This is an excellent primer of Chinese history, including the Boxer Rebellion of 1900, Sun Yat-Sen, and the eventual triumph of Communism in China.   **Upper elem & up**

- **Charles Spurgeon** - Men of Faith Series, by Kathy Triggs
  The story of Charles Spurgeon, one of the greatest preachers in history, is amazing. I loved reading about his gift of humor, his jokes told to school friends over lunch, and his sense of fun. Highly recommended!   **Upper elem & up**

- **Spurgeon - Heir of the Puritans** by Ernest W. Bacon
  Published by Christian Liberty Press, this excellent biography is a deeper look at the foundation of Spurgeon's life. He was known as "the Prince of Preachers," and we would do well to understand his motivations for living to the glory of God. Highly recommended!
  Junior High & up

- **101 Hymn Stories** by Kenneth W. Osbeck
  What a wonderful resource! Though it is not set up chronologically, if you are willing to do a bit of hunting, you will find treasures in the stories of these hymns. This is a marvelous way to bring in another dimension of the story of the Church in history - through the singing of hymns to our Lord. Highly recommended!
  Upper elem & up

- **Fanny Crosby - Writer of 8,000 Songs** by Sandy Dengler
  This is a wonderful biography of an amazing Christian. Fanny Crosby, although blind, became one of the most gifted and treasured hymn writers. Highly recommended!
  Mid elem & up

- **The Hidden Jewel** - Trailblazer Books, by Dave & Neta Jackson
  Historical fiction for children, this is the story of Amy Carmichael and the work she did in India. Highly recommended!
  Mid elem & up

- **Amy Carmichael** - Christian Heroes Then and Now, by Janet & Geoff Benge
  Wonderfully written, this series of Christian biographies is fascinating, factual, and historically accurate. Amy Carmichael was a missionary to India, ending up as "Mommy" to many young Indian orphans who had been rescued from temple prostitution. Highly recommended!
  Mid elem & up

- **Amy Carmichael** - Women of Faith Series, by Kathleen White
  Subtitled, "The Irish missionary to India whose life and writings continue to touch the world," this is a wonderful biography.
  Upper elem & up

- **A Chance to Die - The Life and Legacy of Amy Carmichael** by Elisabeth Elliot
  This is my personal favorite of the Amy Carmichael biographies as Elisabeth Elliot not only tells the story but also challenges us to greater trust in the Lord. Highly recommended!
  Junior High & up

- **A Passion for the Impossible - The Life of Lilias Trotter** by Miriam Huffman Rockness
  Lilias Trotter was a missionary to Muslims in Algeria during the late 1800's and early 1900's. This book tells her fascinating story - including her potential career as a world-class artist which she gave up to go to Algeria.
  Junior High & up

- **John Hyde: The Apostle of Prayer** - Men of Faith Series, by Francis McGaw
  "Praying Hyde" was the name of this missionary who prayed long and hard for India in the late 1800's. Learn more about the results of his prayers in this remarkable little book.
  Upper elem & up

- **John Paton** - Men of Faith Series, by Benjamin Unseth
  The story of a Scottish missionary to the islands of the South Pacific, especially Tanna, this book describes the difficulties early missionaries faced on many of these lovely islands inhabited by cannibals.

- **The Man with the Bird on His Head** - International Adventures,
  by John Rush & Abbe Anderson
  Published by YWAM Publishing, this is one of the most amazing missionary stories of the twentieth century! If you are going to read about John Paton, you MUST read this story, too. It concerns a tribal group on Tanna in the South Pacific who became a "cargo cult" after WWII. They were known as the John Frum people because they were waiting for John Frum to tell them of spiritual truths. (You might enjoy knowing that John Rush is a homeschooling dad.) Absolutely amazing!! Highly recommended!! **Upper elem & up**

- **Carry a Big Stick** - Leaders in Action Series, by George Grant
  Subtitled, "The uncommon heroism of Theodore Roosevelt," this is an amazing biography of an astonishing man. Highly recommended! **Upper elem & up**

- **Theodore Roosevelt: An Initial Biography** by Genevieve Foster
  If you have read any of Genevieve Foster's historical books, you will know that children love her way of presenting history. This is a warm biography of an amazing man.
  Mid elem & up

- **The Story of Thomas Alva Edison** - A Landmark Book, by Margaret Cousins
  The inventions of Thomas Edison changed the entire world! Read about his life and his many inventions, including the phonograph, the electric light bulb, the first motion picture camera, and more in this interesting biography. **Upper elem & up**

- **Alexander Graham Bell** by Patricia Ryon Quiri
  An excellent biography for children, this book tells the story of Bell's life and his wonderful invention - the telephone. **Mid elem & up**

- **Ahoy! Ahoy! Are you there?** - A story of Alexander Graham Bell by Robert Quackenbush
  I love this author! He includes fascinating little tidbits about the people in the time period so that it truly comes alive. **Elementary & up**

- **Around the World in Eighty Days** by Jules Verne
  Classic literature concerning a British gentleman who travels around the world, this book is a wonderful glimpse into the time period. One of my absolute favorites!
  Junior High & up

- **Dates with Destiny - The 100 Most Important Dates in Church History**
  by A. Kenneth Curtis, J. Stephen Lang, and Randy Petersen
  Beginning with the year 64 in Rome and continuing to 1976, this book is filled with short descriptions of events and people within the Church. For this chapter read about Hudson Taylor, Charles Spurgeon, D.L. Moody, William Booth, and the Student Volunteer Movement. Highly recommended! **Upper elem & up**

- **From Jerusalem to Irian Jaya - A Biographical History of Christian Missions**
  by Ruth A. Tucker
  This is the best book on the history of world missions available. Included are short biographies of missionaries all over the world, categorized by their geographical area of service. I consider this an indispensable resource for the study of **World Empires, World Missions, World Wars**. For this chapter read pages 165 - 241. Highly recommended!
  Upper elem & up

Talk Together

Edison and his Phonograph

- Listen to **What in the World's Going On Here?, Volume Two**, tape two, side two. What was the most interesting aspect to you of Prussian nationalism? - The Salvation Army? - The China Inland Mission? Why? What other questions about this time period would you like to have answered?
  History Journal: Write those questions down and, as you study more material, write the answers to your questions. Also, write short bios of the people you study whom you find interesting. Illustrate the bios.

- Why do you think European missionaries were so shocked by Hudson Taylor donning Chinese clothing? What effect do you think this action had on the Chinese people? What essential differences do you think this shows between Hudson Taylor's idea of missions and the previous European missionaries' ideas?

- Why do you think Hudson Taylor lived a spartan lifestyle in England, trusting God to provide all of his needs, when he could have lived in much more luxury and ease? Do you think the lessons he learned in England made a significant difference to his missionary endeavors in China? If you were planning to go as a missionary, would you think it valuable to learn this lesson like Hudson Taylor?

- Define Hudson Taylor's concept of "living by faith." Why did Hudson Taylor and the China Inland Mission choose to be a "faith" mission? What circumstances made this a good decision? Is this still a valid way to live today? Why or why not?

- Why do you think it was difficult for the established churches in England to work with the poor people in the slums? What hindrances were in the way? What do you think were the needs of the poor people in England during the mid-1800's? How were these needs different from the upper and middle classes?

- Why do you think the Salvation Army was so successful at meeting the needs of the "down and outers"? What was the value in preaching in theaters and factories? What purpose do you think the musical bands had? Imagine you had been living in England during this time. Would you have thought the Salvation Army to be a "proper" ministry? Why or why not?

- William Booth's book, **In Darkest England, and the Way Out**, shocked the English public into an awareness of the social needs of the poor of the country. How did this book help the Salvation Army to fulfill their goals of caring for the poor?

- Why do you think the Franco-Prussian War of 1870 was important? What happened to Prussia after the successful conclusion of the war? What happened to France? Do you think that Napoleon III's use of soldiers in Mexico during the period of Maximillian's Empire effected his ability to fight the Franco-Prussian War? Why or why not?

- What was the benefit to Prussia of forming the new German Empire? What was the benefit to the other German states? How do you think the rest of Europe viewed this alliance? Since von Bismarck had shown himself to be a very powerful man, and his policy was "blood and iron," what effect do you think he had on international diplomacy during his tenure as Prime Minister of the German Empire?

- The Student Volunteer Movement was a significant force for missions among university students. The Cambridge Seven went to China in 1885 as "firstfruits" of this move of God. Why do you think these seven men had such a tremendous impact on England when they left for missionary service? Do you see a correlation between this and the Northfield Conference Revival of 1886? What would the effect have been for the churches in 1886 in North America at seeing one hundred university students volunteering for missions?

- Why do you think John Hyde ("Praying Hyde") began to make prayer his full-time missions work? What was the effect of this? Does this seem an unusual way for a missionary to spend his time? Do you think it would be harder to spend your days praying than to spend your days going out among the people? Why or why not?

- Amy Carmichael went to India as a missionary, and found herself taking care of children rescued from the Hindu temples. Do you think this was what she had in mind when she went to India? Why might God have chosen Amy Carmichael as His vessel for ministering to these children - how did her childhood experiences and character traits prepare her for this challenge? Do you think other people may have considered this to be a waste of time? Can you think of any modern day parallels?

- What was the Spanish-American War of 1898 about? Why did America go to war on behalf of the Cubans? Why did Spain go to war over Cuba? What was the outcome of the war?

- Teddy Roosevelt became a national hero during the Spanish-American War. Why do you think he was such an interesting figure to so many people? What were some of his other exploits that made him seem larger than life?

Teaching Time!

Seminar Outline

I. China Inland Mission
    A. Hudson Taylor (1832-1905)
    B. Converted at age 17, felt Lord's call to China
    C. Sailed for China - 1853
    D. Taiping Rebellion (started by a Christian)
    E. Determined to live by faith
    F. Dressed in Native Costume
    G. Married Maria Dyer - 1858
    H. Started China Inland Mission - first faith mission - 1865
        1. Workers and finances prayed in
        2. Supported by George Muller for several years

II. Salvation Army
    A. Revival in USA, 1857 - 50,000 converted per month
    B. Revival in Ireland, 1859, spread to Britain
    C. William Booth (1829-1912) - preacher working during revival
        1. Left established church to work with poor people in slums - 1865
        2. Chose the name of Salvation Army - 1878
        3. Used bands, visited taverns, jails, preached in theaters, factories
    D. International in scope (America, France, India...)
    E. Social relief and rehabilitation

III. Franco-Prussian War of 1870
    A. Emperor Napoleon III of France (Second Empire!)
    B. Von Bismarck - "Blood and Iron"
    C. Telegram sent to Prussia
    D. Insulted the French
    E. War declared on July 19
    F. General von Moltke, head of Prussian Army
    G. French unprepared
        1. Napoleon III taken prisoner at Sedan, deposed, end of 2nd Empire
        2. Paris defeated, early 1871
    H. Treaty of Frankfurt
        1. France gave up most of Alsace-Lorraine (rich mining province)
        2. Had to pay Germany one billion dollars - paid it off in 3 years!
    I. Germany formed German Empire
        1. Kaiser Wilhelm I
        2. Von Bismarck as Prime Minister

IV. Student Volunteer Movement
    A. YMCA started in England by George Williams - 1844
    B. D.L. Moody (1837-1899)
        1. Toured England 1873-1875

       2. Became an internationally known figure

   C. Keswick Convention begins in England - 1875

   D. Cambridge Seven to China - 1885

   E. Northfield Conferences - 1886

       1. Revival

       2. 100 student volunteers for mission field

       3. Begin Student Volunteer Movement in America

V. Missionaries in India

   A. John Hyde ("Praying Hyde") goes to India - 1892

   B. Amy Carmichael (1864-1951) to India - 1895

       1. Founder Dohnavur Fellowship - more than 1,000 children

       2. Served 56 years without furlough

VI. Teddy Roosevelt - (1858-1919)

   A. Worked for two years as a cattle rancher in the Dakota Territory

   B. Went back to the East - worked for the government

   C. Spanish/American War - 1898

       1. Cubans rebelled against Spain

       2. America sided with Cubans

       3. Spanish blew up an American ship in Cuba - "Remember the Maine"

       4. Teddy and his Rough Riders

          a. Teddy became hero

       5. Made governor of State of New York

       6. McKinley asked him to be his Vice-President - 1900

          a. six months later, President assassinated

       7. Teddy made president

          a. Panama Canal

          b. Trust Buster

          c. "Square deal" for miners

          d. First American to win Nobel Peace Prize

          e. "Speak softly and carry a big stick!"

Timeline

On your timeline, mark Hudson Taylor, the start of the China Inland Mission, William and Catherine Booth, the Salvation Army, von Bismarck, the Franco-Prussian War, Kaiser Wilhelm I, Louis Pasteur, D. L Moody, John Hyde, Amy Carmichael, Alexander Graham Bell, Thomas Edison, Teddy Roosevelt, the Spanish-American War.

Research & Reporting

- Find one of the books listed at the beginning of this unit, along with the encyclopedia or other history resource book, for basic information on Otto von Bismarck and the German Empire. Write a report detailing the rise of this powerful leader, his political theories (realpolitik), and the impact of the second German Empire.

- Research and report on the Franco-Prussian War of 1870. What was the Ems telegram? Why did it provoke the war? Show the significance of this war for Prussia and for France.

- In 1853, Hudson Taylor sailed for China which was newly opened to missionaries at the end of the Opium War. Research and report on the causes of the Opium War between China and Great Britain. Who won the war and what benefits did this bring? What happened to the loser?

- Research and report on the Boxer Rebellion. Why was the Dowager Empress of China a supporter of this rebellion? Who were the targets of the Boxer Rebellion? What was the overall effect of this rebellion?

- Research and report on the life and ministry of Hudson Taylor. Describe his childhood, life in London, ministry in China, marriage to Maria Dyer, "living by faith," and the obstacles he overcame.

- Study and describe the China Inland Mission. How did it come into being? What were the defining characteristics of this mission? What kind of people went to China with this organization? How effective was it in bringing the Gospel to the Chinese?

- Research and report on the Salvation Army. Describe its beginning, its leaders, its area of influence, and its purpose. What strategies for ministry were unique (in this time) to this organization?

- Research and report on William and Catherine Booth. Show how they were uniquely qualified to their ministry. Describe their children, and the part they played in the Salvation Army. How did this ministry effect the family?

- The life of D. L. Moody is an interesting one to study. Read about his background, education, and ministry. Write a paper describing his focus in ministry and the opportunities he had to preach the Gospel. What were some of the effects of his ministry (in missions, education, evangelism, etc.)?

- Research and report on the Student Volunteer Movement which began in the 1880's. What caused this? Who was effected? What did they do? What were the results in their own nations? What were the results around the world?

- Research and report on the life of John Hyde. Describe the state of missions in India at the time he went there. What happened after his arrival? What changes did he make? What effect did these changes have?

- Amy Carmichael continues to be an influence throughout the Christian church because of her life and writings. Study and write about her ministry in India and about Dohnavur Fellowship. Describe her commitment to India and its children.

- Research and report on the Spanish-American War. Show where Teddy Roosevelt collected the soldiers who became known as the Rough Riders. Describe the military engagements of this war. What were the results of this war for Spain? - For Cuba? - For the U.S.?

- Louis Pasteur was one of the greatest scientists of all time. Research and report on his life and work. List his major discoveries. How have these affected us today?

- Charles Spurgeon, the "Prince of Preachers," preached in London to huge crowds. Research and report on the life of Spurgeon, and on what factors drew so many to him during a time of decline in church attendance.

- Study and write about the life of Fanny Crosby, the woman hymn writer whose heartfelt words continue to bear fruit. How did her blindness affect her abilities to minister? Describe her life, her gift for remembering poetry, and the process by which she wrote more than 8,000 songs.

- Research and report on the life and discoveries of Thomas Edison. Describe his childhood, his schooling, his scientific inquiries. What obstacles did he overcome?

- Research and report on the life and inventions of Alexander Graham Bell. Where was he born? When did his family move to Canada? What was the reason? How did he become interested in inventing the telephone? What obstacles did he overcome?

- Research and report on the life of Theodore Roosevelt. During his tenure as president, he was involved with several international situations including the Panama Canal and the Russo-Japanese War of 1904-1905. Describe his childhood, his "Wild West" experiences, his military and diplomatic accomplishments, and his "trust buster" activities.

- Research and report on the beginnings of the Y.M.C.A. Where was it started? What were the original purposes of this group?

Brain Stretchers

- Compare and contrast Napoleon III, Klemens von Metternich and Otto von Bismarck. One author, T.A.B. Corley, stated that there was the age of Metternich, followed by the age of Napoleon III and the age of Bismarck. How did their international diplomatic policies affect Europe? Detail the state of affairs in Europe during their time of influence - war? - peace? - alliances? What caused each of them to fall from a position of power? How was Europe affected, first, by the institution of their policies and, second, by the cessation of their policies?

- Research and report on the military strategies used by the Prussian army to defeat Napoleon III and the French Empire. Describe how Napoleon III had used his army prior to this war, then contrast this with how von Bismarck had prepared his army prior to the war. Show the results of this victory for Prussia; show the results of this loss for France.

- Research and report on the Taiping Rebellion including the conditions of life for the Chinese people during the late period of the Manchu dynasty. What were the issues of the Taiping Rebellion? Did it resolve these issues? What was the overall impact of this rebellion?

- Read about John Paton, the missionary to cannibals in the South Pacific. Describe his ministry, and the obstacles he overcame. Compare and contrast his ministry with the story of John Rush, the young man who, in the early 1990's, had an unexpected ministry to tribal people on the island of Tanna - the same island from which John Paton had fled.

Vocabulary

realpolitik	pasteurization	vaccines	cannibals	phonograph
telephone	ethnocentric	spartan	empire	faith mission
exploits	foreign legion	intercession	depose	rehabilitation
furlough	evangelize	missionary	electricity	

Many of the words in this unit have to do with missionaries and their work, and scientists with their inventions.

- Your assignment is to collect as many missionary and scientific terms as you find in this unit's study, and define th

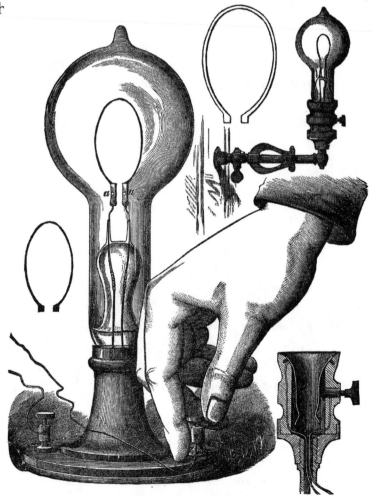

Edison's Incandescent Lamp

Hands On!

**Maps
and
Mapping**

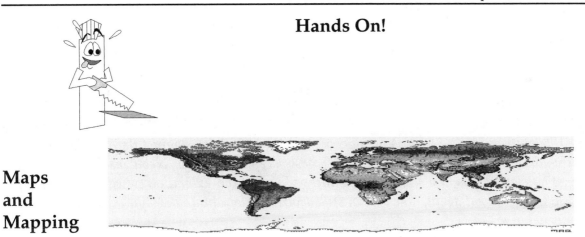

- Using an atlas, encyclopedia, or other resource locate Prussia and these Chinese cities: Shanghai, Ningpo, Yangchow, Hangchow.

- What are the names of the cities and countries that today occupy the same area? What is the capital city, religion, population, major export, and type of government in each modern country? What is the status of Christianity in these countries?

- On a clean worksheet map, draw lines tracing the expansion of the China Inland Mission, the area of Amy Carmichael's ministry in India, and shade in the nations affected by the student Volunteer Movement.

- On another clean worksheet map, draw the expansion of the Prussian nation into the German Empire. Show what area of France was lost to the Germans after the Franco-Prussian War.

- Consult a relief map to discover the terrain found in China. Are there deserts, forest, mountains, islands? Label them. What kind of climate is typical in each of the different terrains? How did these different terrains and climates effect the work of the China Inland Mission?

- Consult a relief map to discover the terrain found in Prussia. Are there deserts, forest, mountains, islands? Label them. What kind of climate is typical in each of the different terrains? How did these different terrains and climates effect the development of the German Empire and of the Franco-Prussian War?

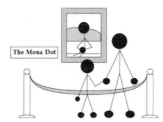

The Mona Dot

Art Appreciation

After the mid-1800's, there was a revolt on the part of many French artists against the strictly controlled, ultra-conservative Academy of Fine Arts whose accepted style was Neo-Classicsm. This rebellion against official art was first seen in the paintings hung at the exhibition called the"Salon of the Rejected" in 1863. This revolt against the official style of art developed into the style of painting known as "Impressionism."

Part of this revolution in art stemmed from a rejection of progress, a rejection of faith in scientific rationalism and materialism, a rejection of the accomplishments of the Industrial Revolution. Rather than continue to follow traditional art styles, the Impressionists rejected the old forms and sought new, modern ways in their art.

This hunger to be "modern" was expressed by Matthew Arnold in his "Essays in Criticism" (1865): "Modern times find themselves with an immense system of institutions, established facts, accredited dogmas, customs, rules, which have come to them from times not modern. In this system their life has to be carried forward; yet they have a sense that this system is not of their own creation, that it by no means corresponds exactly with the wants of their actual life, that, for them, it is customary, not rational. The awakening of this sense is the awakening of the modern spirit. The modern spirit is now awake almost everywhere..."

The first and most important of the Impressionists was Claude Monet. Monet, along with Pissaro, fled France during the Franco-Prussian War of 1870 and sought refuge in England. Here they saw the works of Joseph Turner and John Constable which encouraged them in the artistic style of nature and light that they had been painting. However, Monet went much further. He believed that the most intense optical sensations became possible when mixed - by the eye! So, he painted masses of flecks of contrasting pure color to be mixed by the eye of the viewer. For instance, a spot of red next to a spot of yellow creates a vivid orange when viewed from a distance. His technique involved expressing both color and light in new ways. His focus was to capture the fleeting moment of time through his art - his "impressions" - rather than focusing on a particular subject or theme.

• Locate one of Claude Monet's paintings. Would you describe his painting as realistic? Why or why not? Why do you think his paintings (as well as the other Impressionists' paintings) where scoffed at originally? How do Monet's paintings differ from Millet's? - From David's? - From Turner's? Considering the history of art, do you think something significant changed in the field of art with the Impressionists? Why or why not?

(Author's note: I have always loved Monet's paintings, but when I saw his actual originals in the National Gallery of Art in Washington D.C. I learned that the original paintings, up close and personal, do not look like the reproductions we find in books and museum prints. Instead, one sees very clearly all of the spots and blotches of paint on the painting which make it very ugly. However, when you stand far across the room and look at the painting, all of the spots merge into colors - as described above.)

Arts in Action

- Try your hand at creating Impressionist art and contrasting it with classical art. Using colored dots (red, yellow, blue) from the store, create an Impressionist image. Cut the dots into halves or fourths if they are too big. You may want to lightly sketch an image, then place the dots inside. Hint: lay the colored dots very near each other so they will blend well, and remember to "mix" your primary colors to achieve the color you want:
   red + yellow = orange
   blue + red = purple
   yellow + blue = green
How far away do you have to stand to be able to recognize the image and the "blended" colors?

- Using crayons, tempera paint, or drawing pens, make a large orange on paper. Use orange crayons, tempera paint, or pen to create the orange. On a second piece of paper, create an "orange" using strokes of red with strokes of yellow next to each one. You may use dots instead of strokes if you prefer. Now, set both pictures up against a wall and move to the other end of the room. (You might need to do this outside.) How far back do you need to go before the red and yellow "orange" becomes orange? Which picture do you prefer? Why? What does it look like close up? Try this experiment with other objects - leaves, flowers, etc., always using pure colors beside each other so they will blend into other shades when viewed from a distance.

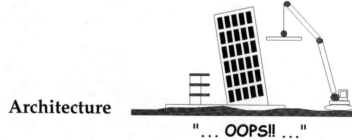

Architecture

"... OOPS!! ..."

Art Nouveau (or "Modern Style") was a style of architecture popular in the late 1800's and early 1900's. It also, like the paintings of the Impressionists, broke away from historical forms and styles. It was originally based on curving lines and vegetation-like forms. Eventually, however, it developed into a style which sought to remove all decoration - in order to express architecturally the "Machine Age."

- Locate a picture of the unfinished Church of the Sagrada Family in Barcelona. Designed by Antoni Gaudi, this church represents the Art Nouveau's "freedom" from historical constraints. The building was developed from the inside outwards, and the decorations were free form.

- The Sezession Building, designed by Joseph Olbrich in Vienna, shows the simple yet non-traditional geometric forms of this developing style. The small amount of ornamentation is based on natural forms (like leaves).

BOOM!!

Science

In 1876, Alexander Graham Bell patented the basic design for a telephone. The ability to use electricity to carry sounds long distances - especially vocal sounds - revolutionized the world. It is important to note that Bell desired to be remembered as a teacher of the deaf rather than the inventor of the telephone!

- Create a "telephone" with two plastic drinking cups and string. Make a small hole in the bottom of each of the cups. Thread the cups onto a long piece of string and tie knots at both ends. Hold one cup to your ear while a second person speaks into the cup. Try this with the string very loose. Can you hear what the person on the other end of the string is saying? Now try this with the string very taut. Can you hear what the person on the other end of the string is saying now? Why do you suppose there is a difference? (Hint: Remember that sound is caused by sound waves or vibrations.)

- In the book, **Make It Work! Sound**, by Alexandra Parsons, there is an experiment for creating a "telephone" with plastic cups, electrical wire, and copper coils. Have fun!

The Bell Telephone

Music

Claude Debussy was one of the most significant composers in music history. He did as much to redirect music as Beethoven. One critic said of Debussy's style, "It is the beginning of the twentieth century breakup of music."

He often wrote music which was as Impressionistic as the French Impressionist painters, like Monet. His music left the traditional forms and structures, the traditional uses of harmony and melody, and moved towards creating an atmosphere of misty, dreamlike sounds. Debussy was an atheist who confessed to having made nature his religion, and, because he was not following God, his music did not follow reasonable, established harmonic practices. He explained that he followed his own rules. His chords sometimes flowed from sound to sound and were only held back from total fragmentation by his masterful musical skill. Though his music is hauntingly beautiful, he was not expressing worship to the one True God.

- Listen to Debussy's "Prelude de l'après midi d'un faune" (1894) ("Prelude to the Afternoon of a Faun"). How would you describe this music? Can you find the theme of the faun which is heard several times during the piece? Would you describe this music as Impressionist? Why or why not? Does it remind you of the Impressionist painters? Explain.

Cooking

With the study of Hudson Taylor and the China Inland Mission, it seemed appropriate to sample a taste of China. Chinese cooking includes many wonderful foods, though it usually requires lots of skill and preparation time. There are relatively few desserts in Chinese cuisine ... but this one is WONDERFUL!

Almond Cookies

2 1/4 cups flour	1 egg
1/8 tsp. salt	1 tsp. almond extract
1 1/2 tsp. baking powder	5 dozen whole blanched almonds
1 cup shortening (like Crisco)	1 egg yolk
1/2 cup granulated sugar	2 Tbsp. water
1/4 cup firmly packed brown sugar	

Preheat oven to 350 degrees. Stir together flour, salt, and baking powder. In a bowl, cream shortening and both sugars until fluffy. Add egg and almond extract; beat until well blended. Add flour mixture and blend well.

Using about 1 tablespoon of the dough each, roll into a ball and place on ungreased baking sheet - 2 inches apart. Flatten each to make a 2-inch round. Press an almond into center of each round. Beat together egg yolk and water; brush over each cookie.

Bake for 10 to 12 minutes, or until lightly browned around edges. Transfer to wire racks and let cool completely. Store in airtight containers. Makes about 5 dozen.

Idea Time

Creative Writing

- Known for your courageous reporting, you have been assigned to interview Otto von Bismarck right after his "Blood and Iron" speech to the Prussian Parliament. Write the story for the "Prussian Press." Remember, of course, that Kaiser Wilhelm supports him enthusiastically.

- Finish this limerick about Alexander Graham Bell:

  There once was a man named Bell
  Who thought it improper to yell...

- Choose three episodes from Hudson Taylor's life and write them into a short, adventure packed story for children.

- The Salvation Army has been gaining a lot of notice in your English city of the late 1800's. Though they have been much maligned recently in the newspaper, you think they are doing a wonderful job for the poor and needy. Write a letter to the editor in their defense. Remember, you want to win people to their cause, so be tactful!

Art

- Draw a political cartoon of the consternation of the French people over the Ems telegram. Be sure to show the Prussian response to this consternation.

Drama

- Dramatize the life and work of Louis Pasteur. Include the discovery of pasteurization, disproving spontaneous generation, etc. The climax should be when he uses his rabies vaccine for the first time on a young boy who will surely die without it.

- Create a Salvation Army band with various members of your family playing appropriate "instruments." Sing or play a few hymns, then have someone preach. Leave one or two people out to be the folks who either respond to the Good News or throw rotten vegies!

The Big Picture

- This unit has been "setting the stage" for the events to come - both in the world and in the church. Prepare, as vignettes, a series of speeches or skits to show the changes that have been wrought during the last part of the 1800's - in Europe, among the poor, in China, among the artists and musicians, and among university students.

Unit Five

The Turn of the Century & The Balkans

The Flight of the Wright Brothers

Unit Objectives:

- To discover the history of the Balkan region and what the impact the Balkan wars had upon the world;

- to learn about Russia at the turn of the century and why it was ripe for revolution;

- to read about the Austrian-Hungarian empire, the Triple Alliance and the Triple Entente Cordiale - the alliances which led to WWI;

- to look at the downward spiral of humanistic philosophies;

- to see God's hand moving in the Welsh Revival of 1904, and the international impact of William Borden's life and death.

Meet the People & Study the Countries:

Here are some people you might meet in this unit:

In the Church:

William Borden   Rees Howells   C. T. Studd
Jonathan Goforth

In the World:

Nicholas II   King George V   Marie Curie
Wright Brothers   Emperor Francis Joseph   Kaiser Wilhelm II

You might wish to study one of these places in depth during this unit:

Austria   Greece   Yugoslavia - Serbia - Croatia
Bosnia-Herzegovina   Albania   Bulgaria
Romania   Wales   Japan (also in Unit 8)

- **The Holy Bible**
  Matthew 5:10-12; Mark 10:28-30; Daniel 2:20-21; Isaiah 60:8; Proverbs 14:12

- **The Twentieth Century** - Cambridge Introduction to the History of Mankind,
  by Trevor Cairns
  This is far and away the best overview of the 1900's that I have seen. Beginning with the early
  1900's attitudes in Europe, Asia, and the U.S., the book includes WWI, the post war conditions,
  WWII, the Cold War, the breakup of colonization around the world, the Korean War, Vietnam,
  and the impact of our technical advances. It also contains detailed charts showing world
  events. Highly recommended!   **Upper elem & up**

- **The Balkans** - Life World Library, by Edmund Stillman
  To study the history of the Balkans is to sort through many conquering countries, rival people
  groups, and various religious enmities. This book is an excellent overview of the history of the
  Balkans.   **High School & up**

- **Yugoslavia** by Carol Z. Rothkopf
  This is a good introduction for children to this very complicated land. It explains the different
  people groups involved, different languages and alphabets, and a bit of the history up to 1971
  (when the book was written).   **Mid elem & up**

- **Yugoslavia** - Enchantment of the World Series, by Carol Greene
  This series of books gives a brief overview of the country's history, its geography, and culture.
  An excellent "primer" for discovering more about Yugoslavia (Serbia/Bosnia-Herzegovina/
  Croatia/Macedonia/Slovinia/Montenegro) and the people of this land.
                                                                 Mid elem & up

- **Albania, Bulgaria, Rumania, Yugoslavia** - The Lands and People of the Balkans, by Dragos D. Kostich
  Excellent for children, this book gives a lot of detail of the history of the Balkans.
  Upper elem & up

- **Greece** - Enchantment of the World Series, by R. Conrad Stein
  This series of books gives a brief overview of the country's history, its geography, and culture. An excellent "primer" for discovering more about Greece and the Greeks.
  Mid elem & up

- **Albania** - Enchantment of the World Series, by David K. Wright
  This series of books gives a brief overview of the country's history, its geography, and culture. An excellent "primer" for discovering more about Albania and the Albanian people. Wonderful photos!
  Mid elem & up

- **Bulgaria** - Enchantment of the World Series, by Abraham Resnick
  This series of books gives a brief overview of the country's history, its geography, and culture. An excellent "primer" for discovering more about Bulgaria and the Bulgarian people.
  Mid elem & up

- **Romania** - Enchantment of the World Series, by Betty Carran
  This series of books gives a brief overview of the country's history, its geography, and culture. An excellent "primer" for discovering more about Romania prior to the fall of Ceausescu.
  Mid elem & up

- **Nicholas II** - World Leaders Past & Present, by George Vogt
  A biography of the last Tsar of all the Russias, this book is a fascinating glimpse into the lives of Nicholas and Alexandra. The errors in judgment, the misguided attempts to rule, and the unwieldy nature of the Russian government under the Tsar are all vividly portrayed. It makes one wonder, "What if ...?"
  Junior High & up

- **Austria** - Enchantment of the World Series, by Carol Green
  This series of books gives a brief overview of the country's history, its geography, and culture. An excellent "primer" for discovering more about Austria and the Austrian people.
  Mid elem & up

- **Austria** - Cultures of the World Series, by Sean Sheehan
  Similar to the series listed above, this book also contains a brief description of the history, geography and culture of Austria. Wonderful pictures!
  Upper elem & up

- **Marie Curie** - People Who Have Helped the World Series, by Beverley Birch
  Subtitled, "The Polish scientist who discovered radium and its life-saving properties," this biography traces the life and scientific work of one of the most amazing scientists in history. Highly recommended!
  Upper elem & up

- **The Story of Madame Curie** by Alice Thone
  This is an excellent biography for younger students to read. Did you know that Marie Curie was Polish, and that because the Russian Tsar had forbidden higher education to Poles, she had to learn about science in secret? (This all changed when she went to Paris to study.)
  Highly recommended!   **Mid elem & up**

- **The Wright Brothers** - The Sower Series, by Charles Ludwig
  Did you know that the Wright brothers were accused of not being the first to invent a flying machine? Read more about this and other details of their amazing invention in this fascinating biography. Highly recommended!   **Upper elem & up**

- **The Wright Brothers** - A World Landmark Book, by Quentin Reynolds
  Well-written and interesting for children, this is the story of the brothers who worked together to make a machine that could fly. Excellent!   **Mid elem & up**

- **Wings - The Early Years of Aviation** by Richard Rosenblum
  What a delightful book! Along with captivating illustrations, this book is filled with fascinating bits and pieces of aviation history. Highly recommended! **Mid elem & up**

- **Cowboys and Kings** by Theodore Roosevelt
  Though this book may be extremely difficult to find (our library had to search through several states!), it is extremely interesting! Ex-president Teddy Roosevelt traveled down the Nile and throughout Europe four years before WWI began. He met the Kaiser (!) and various other European monarchs, and his thoughts about what he saw were candidly written in a letter not intended for publication. Insightful!   **Junior High & up**

- **Incredible Century - A Pictorial History 1901-1970** by R J Unstead
  It is very interesting to see the twentieth century in pictures. This book gives a snapshot look at the major events of the 1900's from a secular perspective. I did not agree with the author's perspective, but a picture IS worth a thousand words!   **Upper elem & up**

- **Borden of Yale** - Men of Faith Series, by Mrs. Howard Taylor
  Subtitled, "The wealthy American whose sacrifice touched Egypt and the world for Christ," this is the story of a young man who counted all things loss for the knowledge of Christ. He went to Egypt in 1913 for language school on his way to China. The untimely death of this fabulously wealthy man electrified the world with the claims of Christ.
  Junior High & up

- **Kim** by Rudyard Kipling
  Set in colonial India, this is Kipling's classic story about a street urchin, the cast off son of a British soldier, and an old Indian man.   **Junior High & up**

- **Mask of the Wolf Boy** - Trailblazer Books, by Dave & Neta Jackson
  This is a historical fiction account of Jonathan and Rosalind Goforth who lived through the Boxer Rebellion in China and went on to see a tremendous response to Jonathan's traveling evangelistic ministry. Excellent!   **Mid elem & up**

- **From Jerusalem to Irian Jaya - A Biographical History of Christian Missions**
  by Ruth A. Tucker
  This is the best book on the history of world missions available. Included are short biographies of missionaries all over the world, categorized by their geographical area of service. I consider this an indispensable resource for the study of **World Empires, World Missions, World Wars**. For this chapter read pages 261 - 288. Highly recommended!
  Upper elem & up

- **Rees Howells - Intercessor** by Norman Grubb
  Deeply impacted by the 1904 Welsh Revival, Rees Howells then went to Africa where he was used mightily by God in revival. The end of the book refers to the dramatic answers to his intercessory prayers during World War II. Life-changing! **Junior High & up**

- **Freckles** by Gene Stratton Porter
  Written at the turn of the century, this is a well-loved story of a young man's life and adventures.
  Great Read Aloud

- **Anne of Green Gables** by L.M. Montgomery
  This classic story of a redhead named Anne should be required reading out loud!
  For the Whole Family

- **Video: The Wind and the Lion**
  This movie concerns an American citizen who was kidnapped in Morocco in the early 1900's. Hollywood substituted "Mrs. Pedicarris" for the actual "Mr. Pedicarris," but, apart from that, it is an intriguing look at international tensions just prior to WWI. Warning: There are two scenes that might be too realistic for younger children.
  Junior High & up

Talk Together

Emperor William

- Listen to **What in the World's Going On Here?, Volume Two**, tape three, side one. What was the most interesting aspect to you of the events leading up to World War One? Why? What other questions about this time period would you like to have answered?
  History Journal: Write those questions down and, as you study more material, write the answers to your questions. Also, write short bios of the people you study whom you find interesting. Illustrate the bios.

- In what ways did the Franco-Prussian War humiliate France? What attitudes do people usually hold about someone who has humiliated them? How would this lead to further conflict?

- If you had been living in England during the time that Prussia formed the second German Empire, what might you have thought about the Germans building up their navy? - What about their colonization in Africa? Why do you think Germany did things that perturbed its European neighbors?

- The Ottoman Empire controlled the Balkan states for hundreds of years. Why do you think the Balkans began to agitate for independence in the 1800's? What other countries might have influenced this? Do you think independence is a desirable thing for a country? Why or why not? Do you think a country's independence is a good thing for the nation that controls that country? Why or why not?

- Historians tell us that Russia was seeking an ice-free port in the Mediterranean. What difference would that have made for Russia? How would that effect the Russian Navy? How would that impact political and military strategies? Why do you think the rest of Europe wanted to prevent that from happening?

- Looking at a map, why do you think Austria-Hungary wanted to occupy Bosnia-Herzegovina? How did this occupation benefit Austria-Hungary? How might this occupation benefit Bosnia-Herzegovina? Do you think Austria-Hungary thought more highly of themselves and their military capabilities than they should have? Why or why not?

- Why do you think Albania declared itself to be a Muslim country? What impact do you think this had on the rest of the Balkan countries? Do you think that the other Balkan countries would tend to be friends or enemies with Albania? Why?

- The Second Balkan War of 1913 made Serbia the "big winner" in the Balkans. Why was this a good news/bad news situation? Who might benefit from Serbian nationalism? Who might be dismayed at the victory of Serbian nationalism?

- In Russia, Tzar Alexander II began reforming the country in the areas of education, freeing the serfs, and beginning local government. Do you think that the radicals who assassinated him realized the impact there would be upon these reforms? Why or why not? When there is a need for change, often there are at least two ways of approaching change - gradually and immediately. What approach do you think the radicals had? What approach did the Tzar have? What do you think might have happened in Russia if the radicals could have joined the Tzar's approach for the good of the country?

- In the Russo-Japanese War of 1904-1905, Russia was defeated by an Asian country that had just recently begun modernizing. Do you think that a defeat at the hands of the Japanese was more damaging to the morale of the Russian government than if they had lost to a European power? Why or why not? What might this defeat have meant to the average Russian citizen?

- Why do you think Japan considered it to be a humiliation when Commodore Perry forced them into a trade agreement with the U.S.? Were the Japanese desirous of trade with foreign powers? Why or why not? Describe how this humiliation effected the goals and strategies of the Japanese government. Do you see any similarity between the military stance of Japan and that of Germany? Describe the similarities.

- How does Picasso's cubist painting, "Les Demoiselles d'Avignon," portray the humanistic philosophies of the time? Why do you think there is an increasing sense of hopelessness and meaninglessness among philosophers? Whatever happened to the ideas of man's basic goodness and the triumph of human reason? (Hint: Consider the French Revolution.)

- Why do you think William Borden's decision to go as a missionary to the Muslims of China caused such consternation in America? Do you think it is unusual that someone who stands to inherit millions of dollars would leave it all behind to go to the mission field? Why or why not? How did his death in Egypt during language school affect the world? What two things had Borden prepared before his death that would help in preaching the gospel to Muslims? What was used to communicate the Gospel after his death? Do you think his life was wasted? Why or why not?

- Why was a "balance of power" so important in Europe? What was Napoleon's role in creating a need for this balance? Why do you think the Triple Alliance and Triple Entente had formed, each with its own particular membership? (Hint: Consider who had been old enemies.)

Teaching Time!

Seminar Outline

I. Events leading up to World War One
  A. Franco-Prussian War of 1870
    1. Paris had been captured and defeated
    2. France had to give up Alsace-Loraine
    3. France had to pay German Empire one billion dollars
    4. France was humiliated and vowed to never let it happen again
  B. Germany was an Empire
    1. Powerful, disciplined army
    2. Built up her navy, threatened England's supremacy on sea
    3. Began colonizing like the other big powers
  C. The Balkans
    1. Ottoman Empire is in decline
    2. Balkan states want independence
      a. Russia wanted an ice-free port
      b. Austria-Hungary wanted to expand
    3. Greece won independence in 1829
    4. Serbia, Romania and Montenegro gain independence in 1878
    5. Bulgaria to govern itself
    6. Austria-Hungary chose to occupy Bosnia-Herzegovina in 1908
    7. Albania and Macedonia were still under Ottoman control.
    8. March 1912, Serbia and Bulgaria made a secret treaty
      a. to attack Turkey
      b. to divide the rest of the Balkans between them
    9. The First Balkan War ended in 1913
    10. Serbia and Bulgaria began divvying up the conquered land
    11. Albania declared itself an independent Muslim principality
    12. Second Balkan War - June 1913
      a. Bulgaria declared war on Serbia and Greece
      b. Bulgaria lost
    13. Treaty of Bucharest - August 1913
      a. Serbia gained a tremendous amount of land
      b. Serbia retained a fierce nationalism
      c. Bosnia-Herzegovina was home to many Serbian nationalists
  D. Russia
    1. After Russia lost the Crimean War
      a. People began questioning their leaders
      b. Tzar Alexander II began reforms
        i. The serfs were freed
        ii. Education improved
        iii. Some local government allowed
      a. Radicals didn't think the reforms went far enough
        i. riots, strikes, violence

         ii. The assassination of the tzar in 1881
- 2. New Tzar Alexander III
  - a. Reversed all of the previous reforms
  - b. Police power increased
  - c. Pressure cooker situation
- 3. Russo-Japanese War (1904-1905)
  - a. Russia is defeated by Japan
  - b. Government shown to be inefficient and harsh
  - c. Workers strike in 1905, troops fired on them, riots broke out.
- 4. New Tzar, Nicholas II (married to Queen Victoria's granddaughter)
  - a. Promises civil rights and a national parliament
  - b. Elections rigged so reformers couldn't get into Parliament
  - c. Opponents arrested
  - d. Leaders of reform movement fled

E. Japan
- 1. Commodore Perry had forced Japan to trade with U.S. - 1853
- 2. England and other nations also wanted trade relation
- 3. Japan humiliated
  - a. determined to become a military and economic power
  - b. In 1868, the Japanese began modernization
    - 1. Goal to become a world power
    - 2. From feudalism to nationalism
    - 3. Militaristic nationalism
- 4. Japanese now placed their loyalty in their nation
- 5. Ruled by a powerful military elite
  - a. Goal - to be as strong and aggressive as possible
- 6. Took Formosa during the wars against China - 1894-1895
- 7. Took part of Manchuria from Russia in the Russo-Japanese War - 1905
- 8. Took Korea

II. Philosophers
A. From bad to worse!
- 1. Optimism of the French Revolution spiraled downward
- 2. Increasing hopelessness, meaningless.

B. Picasso's "Les Demoiselles d'Avignon" - first Cubist Painting - 1907
- 1. Not understandable by reason
- 2. Portrays a new way of thinking

III. The Church
A. Welsh Revival of 1904

B. William Borden
- 1. Student Volunteer Movement
- 2. To minister to Muslims in Northern China
- 3. Went to Cairo first to study Arabic
- 4. Died in Egypt shortly after arrival

IV. Balance of Power in Europe
    A. Triple Alliance
        1. Germany (Kaiser Bill)
        2. Austria-Hungary
        3. Italy
    B. Triple Entente (Cordiale)
        1. France
        2. Russia (Nicholas & Alexandra)
        3. Britain

Timeline

On your timeline, mark the Franco-Prussian War of 1870, Greek independence, Serbian independence, Austrian-Hungarian occupation of Bosnia-Herzegovina, First and Second Balkan Wars, Tzar Alexander II, Alexander III, Nicholas II, beginning of Japanese modernization, war between Japan and China for Formosa, Russo-Japanese War, Picasso, Welsh Revival of 1904, William Borden, Triple Alliance, Triple Entente Cordiale.

Research & Reporting

- Find one of the books listed at the beginning of this unit, along with the encyclopedia or other history resource book, for basic information on the Franco-Prussian War, the Balkans, Japan, or Russia just prior to the Communist Revolution. Write a report detailing what you learn with special emphasis on how this country or war was related to World War One.

- Research and report on the fall of the Ottoman Empire. What were the internal reasons for its decline? - The external reasons? Show the attitude of Europe towards the Ottoman Empire, especially concerning their treatment of Christians.

- Study and write or make a chart about the Balkan Wars. Describe the First Balkan War. Who was fighting in this war? - Who won? What was the result? Describe the Second Balkan War. Who was fighting in this war? - Who won? What was the result? Describe the Treaty of Bucharest in 1913.

- Study and write about Nicholas II and Alexandra of Russia. Describe their family, Rasputin and his influence, and the effect Alexandra had on Russian government.

- The development of Japan from a feudalistic society to a modern nation is a fascinating subject to study. Read about the various means used by the Japanese government to make these changes, and then write a report showing how this was accomplished.

- Research and report on Pablo Picasso's life and painting. Show how he developed his style, how it displayed his worldview, and how it affected other painters and the public.

- Research and report on the life of the scientist, Madame Curie. For what did she win two Nobel prizes? What was her field of study? What are some of the ways in which her discoveries have been utilized?

- The Welsh Revival of 1904 had a tremendous effect, not only on individuals, but on whole towns as well. Study and write about the main figures of the revival and the impact it had. Rees Howells was dramatically changed during this time and went on to other fields of service. Write a short biography of his life and ministry.

- Study and write about the life of William Borden. The biography, **Borden of Yale**, is an excellent resource for this report. Name and describe the area of China where Borden intended to minister among the Muslims. What evangelistic ministries have reached out to this people group?

- Research and report on the Triple Alliance and the Triple Entente Cordiale prior to World War One. Describe the form of commitment these alliances held, how they were formed, and what purpose they served.

- Discover more about Orville and Wilbur Wright's flying machine. Write a report on what the Wright brothers did which allowed them to succeed where so many others failed.

- Research and report on the history of aviation. Include the various uses of airplanes in both wartime and peacetime.

- Look up information on the Boxer Rebellion of 1900 in China. Write a report on who was behind this rebellion, why many people in China feared the "foreign devils" enough to kill them, and what the results of this rebellion were.

Brain Stretchers

- Research and report on the Russo-Japanese War of 1904-05. Why was this war fought? Who won? What was the result in Japan? What was the result in Manchuria? What was the result in Russia?

- Compare and contrast Nicholas II with Peter the Great, then compare and contrast Nicholas II with Kaiser Wilhelm II. Show the governing abilities, leadership skills, family relations, military wisdom, diplomatic policies of each. Then evaluate whether Nicholas II could have prevented the revolution in Russia.

Vocabulary

revolution	occupation	alliance	philosophy
airplane	tsar	radium	radioactive
modernizing	humiliate	agitate	independence
ice-free port	serfs	radicals	reform

In this unit there is a great emphasis on countries changing from a centuries-old form of government to something new.

- Your assignment is to collect as many political/governmental terms as you find in this unit's study, and define them.

Hands On!

Maps and Mapping

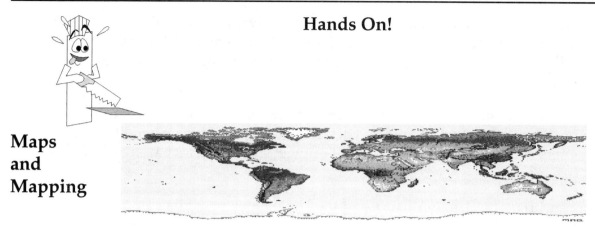

- Using an atlas, encyclopedia, or other resource locate Russia, the Austrian-Hungarian Empire, and the Balkan region.

- What are the names of the cities and countries that today occupy the same area? What is the capital city, religion, population, major export, and type of government in each modern country? What is the status of Christianity in these countries?

- On a clean worksheet map, color in the countries involved in the Balkan Wars. Show the Austrian Empire (including Bosnia-Herzegovina). Also, mark and label the major cities of pre-Communist Russia.

- Consult a relief map to discover the terrain found in the Balkans. Are there deserts, forest, mountains, islands? Label them. What kind of climate is typical in each of the different terrains? How did these different terrains and climates affect the occupation of the various Balkan countries by foreign governments? Was it geographically difficult or easy for the occupying armies?

Art Appreciation

The change made by the Impressionists in art was soon followed by the art of the Post-Impressionists (Gaugin, van Gogh, Cézanne). They were no longer trying to copy nature - even fleetingly - but seeking to create their own expression of reality on the flat surface of the canvas. At the turn of the century, the works of these artists, who had been relatively unknown before this, were introduced to a whole new group of young painters. The results were cataclysmic - catapulting art into twentieth century, modern art.

The forerunner of all modern art was Picasso's "Les Demoiselles d'Avignon," painted in 1907. He captured the spirit of the age with the dehumanizing of humanity in this "cubist" style. In **Modern Art and the Death of a Culture**, *H. R. Rookmaaker states,*
"So, this is an art which is definitely not naturalistic. It seeks the general, the universal. It tends towards abstraction, even towards the demonic. It loses a humanist humanity, and is at the same time both extremely intellectual and irrational. In short it sums up all aspects of modern art at the very moment that it was born."

- Find one of Picasso's cubist paintings. How would you describe it? Cézanne, in a letter to another painter, said, "Treat nature by the cylinder, the sphere, the cone, all brought into perspective." Do Picasso's paintings seem to reflect this advice?

Arts in Action

In the continuing search for ways to express the absurdity and fragmentation of twentieth century life, the cubist artists began experimenting with adding materials to the canvas - such as newsprint, cardboard, wallpaper - in a style called "collage."

Though we reject the non-Christian worldview expressed in modern art, we can use this art form to show how fragmented the post-Christian world has become.

- Create a collage of local, national and/or international events from the newspaper - in the style of the cubists. Cut out several portions of pictures or portions of articles in geometric shape. Paste the newspaper shapes in random arrangement on poster board. You may wish to add lines of color. Be sure to assign an appropriate title so people will know what your collage is about! Now, with your family, evaluate what you have created. Does it convey a story? Is it hard to understand? Is it helpful, worthwhile, enjoyable to look at? Would this art form be a good representation of the fragmentation of modern life without Christ? Why or why not?

- To contrast the above project, try creating a picture or diorama of a story that has meaning to your family. Make it is as understandable and clear as possible. Assign a title if necessary. Now, with your family, evaluate what you have created. Does it convey a story? Is it hard to understand? Is it helpful, worthwhile, enjoyable to look at? Would this art form be a good representation of the Christian life? Why or why not? How does this differ from the collage?

"... OOPS!! ..."

Architecture

The architecture of Frank Lloyd Wright (1869-1959) was exhilarating to the architects of Europe when they first saw his designs published in the Wasmuth publications of 1910 and 1911. His "Robie House" in Chicago, appeared exotic, almost Japanese, to the Europeans. Alan Bowness, in **Modern European Art***, writes,*
"The wide-spreading, hipped roofs and continuous strips of windows give it a low, horizontal emphasis. There is no ornamentation of any kind, nothing to detract from the impact of the building's sculptural forms... The plan, with its multiple levels and easy flow between the rooms confirms this aspect of spatial freedom. Wright's innovations make an interesting parallel with those of the cubist painters in this same year."

- Locate a picture of Wright's "Robie House," or one of his other "prairie" style houses. How is this architecture different from the architecture of the 1800's? How is it like "cubism"?

BOOM!!

Science

The world's first powered flight took place on December 17, 1903 at Kittyhawk, North Carolina. Who were the two men responsible? Orville and Wilbur Wright. Their story is one of amazing creativity, invention, ingenuity, and perseverance. Read more about them!

- Learn about the principle of "lift" which allows heavier-than-air airplanes to stay aloft. Try this: Cut a piece of paper into a two-inch by eight-inch strip. Fold it in half so it is two inches by four inches. Slide one end of the paper one-half inch back, and tape it or glue it to the bottom. One side should be curved and one straight - just like an airplane's wing. Slip the folded end over a pen, hold it up to your mouth and blow on the fold. What happens when you blow? What happens when you stop?

The principle, discovered by Daniel Bernoulli, is that air has less pressure when it is moving. The faster it moves, the less pressure it exerts. When you blow air across the fold, the curve in the paper makes the air go further and faster than on the straight underside of the paper. This means that there is less pressure on the top (moving faster over the curve) and more pressure on the bottom. That's what keeps a plane in the air!

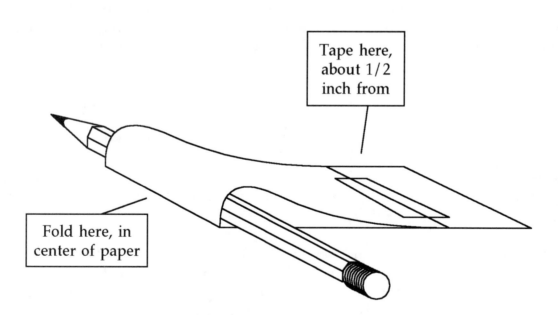

Tape here, about 1/2 inch from

Fold here, in center of paper

Music

Igor Stravinsky's early compositions were the start of twentieth century music. According to Grout, they "... exemplify nearly every significant musical tendency of the first half of the twentieth century." With "The Firebird," "Petrouchka," and "Rite of Spring" - three of the most influential compositions from the turn of the century - Stravinsky's audiences were startled by the rhythmic drive and difficulty, the dynamic extremes, the unfamiliar melodic structure, and the powerful orchestral effects. These extremes in compositional style and orchestration became the new standard for the next three decades.

- Listen to "The Rite of Spring" ("Le Sacre du Printemps") or "Petrouchka" by Stravinsky. Can you understand the dramatic breakoff between this music and that of Debussy or other composers of the nineteenth century? What words could you use to describe this music? (If your student is not familiar with the sounds of the experimentation or with the strident harmonies and rhythmic effects which twentieth century composers have been utilizing, then they will most likely be startled by the sound of Stravinsksy's music - much as the Parisian audiences of 1910-1913.)

- For further study in this time period, listen to ragtime music by Scott Joplin, especially "Maple Leaf Rag" or "The Entertainer."

Cooking

This is an unusually tasty way to serve carrots. As you munch, talk about what you have learned of the Balkans.

Balkan Braised Carrots

6 Tbsp. butter	Salt
2 tsp. sugar	Freshly ground pepper
12 carrots, thinly sliced	1 1/2 cup plain yogurt
4 green onions, cut into 1-inch pieces	3 Tbsp. fresh dill, chopped
Cayenne pepper	

Melt the butter in a saucepan. Add the sugar, carrot slices and green onions. Cover and cook gently (braise) until carrots are tender - about 15 minutes. Season to taste with the spices. Add yogurt and dill, heat through (do not allow this to boil). Serve immediately. Serves 6.

Idea Time

Creative Writing

- You are an official observer sent by the English government to report on the Balkan wars. Write short telegrams to send home describing briefly what is taking place between the various countries of the Balkans and the Ottomans. Remember, every word in a telegram is expensive, so be concise!

- You entered the contest, "Meet the Tzarina at Home," and won an all-expenses-paid trip to Russia to meet Nicholas and Alexandra. Write a newsy letter to your parents telling them your observations of the court life of Russia. Be sure to include any concerns you may have about the influence of Rasputin.

- Write a children's story of the Welsh Revival of 1904. (**Rees Howells: Intercessor** is an excellent resource for this) Be sure to tell the story of how policemen in certain towns had nothing to do because there was no crime after the revival!

- Finish this poem about the Triple Alliance and Triple Entente Cordiale:

They called it a "balance of power,"
Which made it a novel idea...

Art

- Draw a political cartoon showing how Russia's interest in gaining an ice-free port caused them to make friendly overtures to Serbia.

Drama

- Dramatize the work of Wilbur and Orville Wright - from the wind tunnel they made in their bicycle shop to the world's first powered flight of an airplane. You might want to do this one with puppets.

- Create a skit which shows the members of the Triple Alliance and the members of the Triple Entente Cordiale. Through the use of drama, show the tensions building between these two groups - and what caused them!

The Big Picture

- To show what is taking place around the world during the early 1900's, plan a "travel lecture" for family, friends and neighbors. You might want to get some travel posters to show the different countries and cities, but then speak about each area as if you were living in 1913. Include Russia, the Balkans, Paris, Wales, Austria-Hungary, German Empire, and England.

Unit Six

WWI & The Bolshevik Revolution

"Time's up - over you go!" - trench warfare

Unit Objectives:

- To study the various aspects of World War I:

    - the war in the trenches

    - the war in the air

    - the war on the sea

    - the new inventions - tanks, chemical warfare;

- to discover the work of T.E. Lawrence in WWI and its impact upon the Arabs;

- to learn about the Bolshevik revolution in Russia and how it changed life for the people.

Meet the People & Study the Countries:

Here are some people you might meet in this unit:

T. E. Lawrence	Chaim Weizmann	Vladimir Lenin
Joseph Stalin	Leon Trotsky	General Pershing
Woodrow Wilson	General von Moltke	Archduke Francis Ferdinand
General Ludendorff	Red Baron	General von Hindenberg

You might wish to study one of these places in depth during this unit:

Saudi Arabia	Other Arab countries	Russia

Other countries part of the former The Soviet Union

- **The Holy Bible**
  Psalm 27:1-3, 46:8-9, 140:1-2; Proverbs 15:22, 22:24-25; James 4:1-2

- **The Twentieth Century** - Cambridge Introduction to the History of Mankind, by Trevor Cairns
  This is far and away the best overview of the 1900's that I have seen. Beginning with the early 1900's attitudes in Europe, Asia, and the U.S., the book includes WWI, the post war conditions, WWII, the Cold War, the breakup of colonization around the world, the Korean War, Vietnam, and the impact of our technical advances.   It also contains detailed charts showing world events.   Highly recommended!   **Upper elem & up**

- **The Story of the First World War** by Colonel Russell Reeder
  My first choice for a "primer" of WWI, this book explains, through interesting stories, the various details of fighting a war on two fronts with many nations involved. Highly recommended!   **Upper elem & up**

- **World War I** - Wars that Changed the World Series, by Ken Hills
  This is an excellent "primer" of WWI for younger children, and is filled with illustrations.   **Mid elem & up**

- **World War I** - America's Wars Series, by Gail B. Stewart
  This is a description of WWI from the perspective of the Americans. It shows the war effort (including no longer permitting steel ribs to be used in corsets!), the relationship between the Kaiser and President Wilson, and the impact of the U. S. entering the war on the side of the Allies.   **Upper elem & up**

- **World War One - An Illustrated History in Colour 1914-1918** by Robert Hoare
  If you can find this book, it will be worth its weight in gold! Filled with pictures, maps, brief descriptions of different facets of the war, this is a fantastic overview of the "war to end all wars." Highly recommended!   **Upper elem & up**

- **America's First World War: General Pershing and the Yanks** - A World Landmark Book by Henry Castor
  Fascinating! This biography is about the man in charge of the American soldiers sent to Europe in WWI. His job was not enviable - bringing the "doughboys" up to battle standards and making sure they were adequately led and adequately provisioned. Highly recommended! **Upper elem & up**

- **The World War I Tommy** - The Soldier through the Ages Series, by Martin Windrow
  This is a very concise, simple look at the different parts of World War I, written and illustrated for children. It would make an excellent primer of the war for elementary students. **Mid elem & up**

- **In Flanders Fields - The Story of the Poem by John McCrae** by Linda Granfield
  This is the best children's book I have seen about the realities of fighting in World War One. It is not so graphic that children would have nightmares, but it does convey the sense of horror and loss for the soldiers in this war. It is worth searching for! **Mid elem & up**

- **Wings - The Early Years of Aviation** by Richard Rosenblum
  What a delightful book! With captivating illustrations, this book is filled with fascinating bits and pieces of aviation history. Highly recommended! **Mid elem & up**

- **Flying Aces of World War I** - A World Landmark Book, by Gene Gurney
  This book contains fascinating accounts of the best fighter pilots of several nations during the first war to use airplanes - WWI. Meet the men who changed the nature of battles with the use of their machines. Absolutely riveting. **Upper elem & up**

- **Sky Battle: 1914 - 1918** by David C. Cooke
  This is the story of the development of the airplane as a weapon of war - from the spindly contrivance of wood and muslin found in the first airplanes to deadly machines. Well-written and well-researched. **Upper elem & up**

- **Saudi Arabia** - Enchantment of the World Series, by Leila Merrell Foster
  This series of books gives a brief overview of the country's history, its geography, and culture. An excellent "primer" for discovering more about Saudi Arabia and the Arabian people. It will help your students to understand more about the impact of WWI and T.E. Lawrence on the Arabs. **Mid elem & up**

- **Lawrence of Arabia** - A World Landmark Book, by Alistair MacLean
  This is everything you would expect from this author about this person! T.E. Lawrence was one of the most significant military minds of WWI. Though he labored in a war far from the European trenches and without important military rank, yet his actions on behalf of the Arabs of Mesopotamia helped to defeat the Turkish and German Empires. Absolutely fascinating! Highly recommended. **Upper elem & up**

- **Chaim Weizmann** - World Leaders Past & Present, by Richard Amdur
  This is the biography of a Russian Jew who studied science in Germany, moved to England, and, by his scientific assistance to the British during WWI, gained the Balfour Declaration of 1917 - which guaranteed the Jews a national homeland in Palestine. Chaim Weizmann, a fascinating personality, was the first elected president of the new nation of Israel. Highly recommended! **Junior High & up**

- **Russia** - Cultures of the World, by Oleg Torchinsky
  This series for children includes a brief description of the history, geography and culture of a country. In this book, learn more about Russia and the Russian people. Since it was written after the breakup of the U.S.S.R., it includes information about the current situation. Fascinating! **Upper elem & up**

- **The First Book of the Soviet Union** by Louis L. Snyder
  This is an excellent book for introducing to children the history of Russia and the Communist Revolution. It includes a fascinating description of Lenin's return to Russia through German lines. Highly recommended! **Upper elem & up**

- **Russia** - Festivals of the World Series, by Harlinah Whyte
  This fun children's book includes a craft project of making "babushka" dolls - a traditional Russian toy. **Mid elem & up**

- **The Union of Soviet Socialist Republics** - Enchantment of the World Series, by Abraham Resnick
  This series of books gives a brief overview of the country's history, its geography, and culture. An excellent "primer" for discovering more about Russia and the Russian people. It was written before the breakup of the U.S.S.R. **Mid elem & up**

- **Vladimir Lenin** - World Leaders Past & Present, by John Haney
  This biography of the man who brought communism to Russia puts together all of the elements involved - his exile, the provisional government set up after the abdication of the Tsar, the "Red Revolutionaries" fighting the "White Revolutionaries," the October Revolution, and more. **Junior High & up**

- **Joseph Stalin** - World Leaders Past & Present, by Dorothy and Thomas Hoobler
  The successor to Lenin, Stalin is the man who said, "The greatest delight is to mark one's enemy, prepare everything, avenge oneself thoroughly, and then go to sleep." His purge of the Soviet Union cost more than 300,000 lives. This book tells his story. **Junior High & up**

- **Leon Trotsky** - World Leaders Past & Present, by Hedda Garza
  This man was one of the two pivotal figures in the 1917 October Revolution in Russia. Learn in this fascinating biography how Stalin displaced Trotsky after Lenin's death, and why Stalin later had him murdered. (Parents, please read this book to decide if it is appropriate for your students.) **Junior High & up**

- **Incredible Century - A Pictorial History 1901-1970** by R.J. Unstead
  It is very interesting to see the twentieth century in pictures. This book gives a snapshot look at the major events of the 1900's from a secular perspective. I did not agree with the author's perspective, but a picture IS worth a thousand words!   **Upper elem & up**

- **Dates with Destiny - The 100 Most Important Dates in Church History**
  by A. Kenneth Curtis, J. Stephen Lang, and Randy Petersen
  Beginning with the year 64 in Rome and continuing to 1976, this book is filled with short descriptions of events and people within the Church. For this chapter read about the publications of The Fundamentals, which launched the fundamentalist movement. Highly recommended!   **Upper elem & up**

- **Cheaper by the Dozen** by Frank B. Gilbreth, Jr. and Ernestine Gilbreth Carey
  Efficiency! That's the word around which this American family functions. A classic!
                                                                        Great Read Aloud

- **The Secret Adversary** by Agatha Christie
  Dame Agatha writes a mystery about Tommy and Tuppence which begins with the sinking of the Lusitania. A classic mystery.   **Upper elem & up**

- **Video: Sergeant York**
  The true story of Sergeant York is amazing! As a Christian, he was not sure that it was right to go off to war. The movie shows how he resolved this issue, and what the incredible results were. Highly recommended!   **For the whole family.**

- **Video: Lawrence of Arabia**
  This award-winning movie is an excellent depiction of T. E. Lawrence and the Arabs who fought against the Germans in WWI. However, there are some graphic depictions of violence and the movie leaves you with the impression that Lawrence was insane at times. His family disagreed with the interpretation of the director. Having said all that, it is still worth watching.   **Junior High & up**

Talk Together

Prince Ferdinand of Austria

- Listen to **What in the World's Going On Here?, Volume Two**, tape three, side two. What was the most interesting aspect to you of World War One that was mentioned? Why? What other questions about this time period would you like to have answered?
  History Journal: Write those questions down and, as you study more material, write the answers to your questions. Also, write short bios of the people you study whom you find interesting. Illustrate the bios.

- Why do you think a Serbian nationalist assassinated the Archduke Francis Ferdinand? What do you suppose he hoped to accomplish through this violent act? What were the attitudes of the Serbians towards Austria-Hungary?

- Why did Austria declare war against Serbia rather than Bosnia-Herzegovina (where the Archduke was assassinated)? What do you think Austria hoped to accomplish?

- Why did Russia mobilize its troops? Why did Germany declare war on Russia? Why did Germany declare war on France? Why did Great Britain declare war on Germany?

- Why do you think the Germans invaded Belgium? (Hint: Look at a topo-graphical map.) What was the result?

- Why did Serbia come into the war on the side of the Allies? Why did the U.S. come into the war on the side of the Allies? Why do you think Italy changed sides and came into the war on the side of the Allies? Why did Bulgaria come into the war on the side of the Central Powers? Why did the Ottoman Empire come into the war on the side of the Central Powers?

- The "German wheel" strategy for quickly conquering France had been planned for nine years prior to the war. Why do you think von Moltke changed the plan at the last minute? What was the result? What do you think would have happened if the Germans had been successful?

- Why do you think that each side had the soldiers dig trenches? What caused this change in military tactics? (Hint: Consider the change in weapons and technology.) How did this change the way war was fought? Describe what you know of previous military tactics, then discuss whether WWI were a different kind of war.

- Why do you think the Russian generals in charge of the two main armies of Russia chose not to work with each other? What was the result? How was this different from the generals commanding the German armies? What attitude do you think the Russian military had towards the Germans? Why do you suppose they held this attitude? What were the results?

- What do you think the tremendous losses to the Russian armies did to the people back home in Russia? How might this have affected economics, politics, attitudes? As you read more about Tsar Nicholas II, examine how he chose to deal with this situation. Was it effective? Why or why not?

- Why did the British set up a naval blockade? What would this do to Germany? What kinds of products, goods or services would not be able to come via ship if there was a blockade? Do you think this was a concern to the Germans? Why or why not? What did the Germans do to retaliate? How effective was this?

- America became the "supply house" for the Allies in Europe during the war. Why did this make them a target for the German submarines? What was the effect of German subs sinking American ships? Do you think the German plan backfired? Why or why not?

- When Winston Churchill was First Lord of the Admiralty, he authorized a plan for the Allies to take the Dardanelles, which would open a direct supply route through the Black Sea to Russia. Australian and New Zealander soldiers fought the Turks at Gallipoli for this purpose, and lost disastrously. Why do you think the Allies considered the resupplying of Russia to be important enough to risk battling on Turkey's "doorstep"?

- Both poison gas and tanks were developed for use in WWI. Why? How were they supposed to "help" the war effort? Did they make a difference?

- Why were airplanes needed for reconnaissance in WWI? How did they develop into aggressive weapons of war? Why did the pilots need a gun that would shoot from the front rather than the sides? What were the difficulties involved in doing this? Which side had this capability first? How did this affect the war in the air? Why do you suppose there was such a long waiting list to become a pilot when the life expectancy for pilots was only 3-6 weeks?

- Why do you think the Tsar relinquished his throne? What effect did this have upon Russia? Upon the revolutionary exiles? Why do you suppose the Tsar did not flee with his family? Do you think this situation is similar to the French Revolution? Why or why not?

- Why do you think Germany helped Lenin to get back to Russia since Germany and Russia were at war? What might they have hoped to receive from Lenin if they helped him? What was the effect of Lenin's return? How did this affect the war on the Eastern Front? How did this affect the war on the Western Front?

- T. E. Lawrence is one of the most interesting personalities of this war. How unusual do you think it was for a British soldier to lead Arab guerrilla fighters? How was Lawrence uniquely qualified to do this work? What do you think Lawrence hoped to accomplish for the Arabs? Do you think the efforts of Lawrence and the Arabs made a difference in the Allied war effort? Why or why not?

- Why do you think General Pershing would not allow American soldiers to fight under French or British commanders? What was the impact of this decision upon the Allies? How long did it take for the Americans to actually begin fighting in the war? Do you think the American presence made a difference to the Allied cause? Why or why not?

- Why do you think the Kaiser abdicated? Did the Germans actually lose the war, or did they just stop fighting? Look up the word "armistice" in a dictionary. What does it mean? How might an armistice possibly have influenced the attitudes of the German military in the era between WWI and WWII?

- Why did the German ambassadors sign the Treaty of Versailles if the terms were so harsh towards Germany? What were their options? Why do you think the Allies, especially France and England, were so vindictive in this treaty? What was the result of this treaty? What do you think might have happened if the terms of the treaty had been more generous towards Germany?

Teaching Time!

Seminar Outline

I. World War One
 A. The Spark - June 28, 1914
  1. In Bosnia-Herzegovina
  2. Archduke Francis Ferdinand assassinated
  3. Committed by a Serbian nationalist, Gavrilo Princip
 B. The Result
  1. Austria declares war on Serbia - July 28, 1914
  2. Russia mobilizes its troops to defend Serbia from Austria
  3. Germany declares war on Russia (Triple Alliance) - August 1, 1914
  4. Germany declares war on Russia's ally - France - August 3, 1914
  5. Germany invades Belgium (a neutral territory) - August 4, 1914
  6. Britain declares war on Germany - August 4, 1914
 C. The Opposing Sides
  1. Allies
   a. Britain
   b. France
   c. Russia
   d. Serbia
   e. Greece
   f. Italy
   g. USA
     i. America's policy of isolation
     ii. Friendly to both Britain and Germany
  2. Central Powers
   a. Germany
   b. Austria-Hungary
   c. Bulgaria
   d. Ottoman Empire
 D. Tactics
  1. German Wheel
   a. Developed by General Alfred von Schlieffen
   b. Changed by General von Moltke in the field
   c. Didn't work
  2. Race to the English Channel
   a. Each army trying to outflank the other
   b. Each side dug trenches
 E. The Western Front -
  1. From Swiss Alps to the English Channel (almost 600 miles)
  2. New kind of warfare
   a. Trench warfare
   b. No-man's land
   c. Defender's war

F. Eastern Front
    1. Russian armies
        a. Commanded by two generals
        b. They hated each other
        c. Worked alone
    2. German armies
        a. Commanded by two generals
            i. Von Hindenburg
            ii. Ludendorff
        b. Worked together
    3. Battle of Tannenberg - August 23, 1914 to August 31, 1914
    4. Battle of Masurian Lakes
    5. Russia defeated in both battles
        a. Russians lost two-thirds of their invading troops
        b. Most of their war supplies
        c. On the defensive now
    6. Russians drove the Austrians back
        a. Austrians could not subdue Serbia
    7. Trenches were dug along the Eastern front
        a. 800 miles of trenches from the Baltic Sea to Rumanian border
        b. Completed by the end of 1914

G. War At Sea
    1. At start of WWI
        a. Britain had 40 battleships
        b. Germany had 33
        c. France had 21
        d. Austria had 13
    2. British Navy cleared the Mediterranean
    3. British Navy closed sea routes from the North Sea to the Atlantic
        a. Blockade against Germany
        b. Keep war supplies or food from reaching Germany
    4. Germany went under the water - U-Boats (submarines)
        a. Announced February 4, 1915, they would attack any vessels, neutral or not, sailing in the waters of the British Isles
        b. Used torpedoes to blow up enemy targets
        c. Lusitania sunk on May 7, 1915, just off the coast of Ireland
            i. Killed 1,198 people
            ii. 128 Americans died
            iii. America outraged
    5. America supplied food and armaments through merchant ships
        a. Germany kept sinking them
        b. America became angry, eventually entering the war

H. New weapons of war
    1. Germans introduce poison gas in battle - April 22, 1915
    2. Britain introduces tanks in battle - September of 1916

I. Battle in the Air
    1. Airplanes used, at first, just for reconnaissance

2. Eventually used in battle
3. Anthony Fokker (in Germany) - 1915
    a. developed machine gun that worked with propellers
    b. Germans became masters of the sky
4. French mechanics discovered secret - 1916
5. Flying extremely dangerous
    a. Average life expectancy of new pilot was between 3 - 6 weeks

II. Revolution in Russia
    A. Peasants revolt - March 15, 1917
        1. Russia is starving
        2. Soldiers are losing
        3. Tsar relinquishes his throne
    B. Lenin
        1. Transported from his exile in Switzerland to Russia
        2. Promises to make peace with Germany
    C. October Revolution - Bolshevik Revolution - Communist Revolution
    D. Russia surrenders to Germany - December 15, 1917

III. America joins the Allies
    A. America declares war on Germany - April 6, 1917
    B. American troops begin landing in France - June 24, 1917
        1. General Pershing kept Americans under American control
            a. French and British desperate
            b. Germans moving troops from Eastern front to Western front
            c. Race to see who can get the most troops to the Western Front
    C. Germans begin their final three offensives - March 21, 1918
    D. American troops in Battle of Belleau Wood - June 6, 1918
    E. Final Allied Offensive - September 2, 1918
    F. American and French force in Argonne Forest - November 3, 1918
    G. Armistice - November 11, 1918
        1. Kaiser flees to Holland
        2. German troops told to lay down arms

IV. End of World War One
    A. Treaty of Versailles - June 1919
        1. Harsh terms
            a. Germany's colonies seized
            b. Allied troops to occupy west of the Rhine River
            c. Germany's navy reduced to six warships, no submarines at all
            d. No heavy artillery
            e. Army limited to 100,000
            f. Germany declared guilty for the war
            g. $33 billion dollars to be paid to Allies
        2. German ambassador forced to sign
            a. Blockade was continuing
            b. German people starving
            c. Armies ready to inflict more punishment
    B. An uneasy peace

Timeline

On your timeline, mark the assassination of Archduke Francis Ferdinand, the mobilization of each nation, WWI, the sinking of the Lusitania, the introduction of poison gas and tanks, Bolshevik Revolution, T.E. Lawrence, Gallipoli, America's entrance into the war, Armistice, Treaty of Versailles.

Research & Reporting

- Find one of the books listed at the beginning of this unit, along with the encyclopedia or other history resource book, for basic information on World War One. Write a report presenting an overview of the war, including the causes of the war, the chronology, the technological developments and the results of the war.

- Research and report on the relationship between Austria-Hungary and Bosnia-Herzegovina. The book, **Cowboys and Kings**, by Theodore Roosevelt, gives a fascinating glimpse into the rigid authoritarian attitude of the Archduke Francis Ferdinand. If you can find this book, analyze how the Archduke would have represented Austrian monarchical rule to the people.

- Make a chart showing the chronology of events at the start of World War One. Be sure to include the entry of each of the European countries into the war, and the development of the first several months of military strategy.

- Research and report on the development of submarines, and their usage in World War One. You may want to create a diagram showing the placement of British warships in the German blockade, and how the German submarines were able to avoid the blockade and wreak havoc among the merchant ships.

- Study and write about the development of the tank during and after World War One. Show why it was needed, what made it uniquely suited to modern warfare, and how it affected World War One and World War Two.

- Research and report about the use of the airplane for military use during and after World War One. Describe the way airplanes became an offensive tool with the addition of machine guns and bombs. Include stories of the pilot "aces" from both sides in the war.

- Research and report on the Allied plan to capture the Dardanelles and the battle at Gallipoli. Include Kemal Ataturk's defense of Gallipoli as well as the gallant attempt to capture it by the soldiers of Australia and New Zealand.

- T.E. Lawrence led the Arabs in revolt against the Ottoman Turks and the Central Powers during World War One. Research and report on his life, his military accomplishments, and the effect Arab successes had on the Middle East during the post-World War One era.

- Study and write about America's involvement in World War One. Show America's merchant supply line to the Allies, and what events brought America into the war as a combatant. Include the way American soldiers were deployed and the timing of this deployment.

- Research and report on the end of World War One. Show what happened to Austria-Hungary, Bulgaria and the Ottoman Empire prior to the Armistice between the Allies and Germany. Describe the Armistice and the Treaty of Versailles. Be sure to include the way many European boundaries were "re-drawn" at the Treaty of Versailles.

- Research and report on the beginning of the "Fundamentalist" movement in the church. Show where the term came from, how it was used, and what was the purpose of this movement.

Brain Stretchers

- Russia entered the war on the side of the Allies. Research and report on what happened to the Tsar's government during the first years of the war, and what happened to Russia after his abdication. Include the fledgling democratic government under Kerensky, and the Bolshevik Revolution under Lenin and Trotsky.

Vocabulary

trenches	tank	chemical warfare	submarine
Bolshevik	aces	aviation	resupply
provisional	exile	abdication	fundamentals
assassinate	mobilize	invade	strategy

In this unit there is a great emphasis on military terminology for WWI.

- Your assignment is to collect as many new military terms as you find in this unit's study, and define them.

Hands On!

**Maps
and
Mapping**

- Using an atlas, encyclopedia, or other resource locate the areas affected by World War One - including all of the countries which provided soldiers - and by the Bolshevik Revolution.

- What are the names of the cities and countries that today occupy the same area? What is the capital city, religion, population, major export, and type of government in each modern country? What is the status of Christianity in these countries?

- On a clean worksheet map, draw lines tracing the Western Front and the Eastern Front, showing the various sites of battles (including Gallipoli). Also, show the area where the Red Russians and White Russians fought during the Bolshevik Revolution.

- Consult a relief map to discover the terrain found in the Western Front, Eastern Front, Dardanelles, and Russia. Are there deserts, forest, mountains, islands? Label them. What kind of climate is typical in each of the different terrains? How did these different terrains and climates affect each side of WWI? How did these different terrains and climates affect the Bolshevik Revolution?

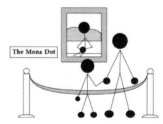

Art Appreciation

During WWI, a group of anti-war, anti-Western civilization artists formed a group with an artistic style known as "Dada" (chosen specifically because it is a meaningless word). This art, according to its inventor, Tristan Tzara, "signifies nothing." However, it powerfully expressed a worldview philosophy of meaninglessness and absurdity, leading eventually to "surrealism."

One of the best-known artists of this style was Marcel Duchamp. He had also painted in the cubist style, but as WWI enveloped much of Europe, he began exhibiting ready-made objects (which he signed, as the artist) to refute the idea of art expressing meaning. According to Alan Bowness, in **Modern European Art***,*
"Such anarchic gestures were appropriate at the height of a world war, when civilized nations seemed to have plunged into an escalating lunacy in which all regard for the very human values they were meant to be defending had been lost. What could the artist do but protest?"

It is important to understand something of this style of art since it was a powerfully influential movement of a number of artists, writers and philosophers in the early twentieth century.

- Look up "Dadaism" in the encyclopedia. The photo showing Dada art will give you a sense of this meaningless and absurd style. Does the title have anything to do with what is there? How would you describe this "work of art"? How does this art truly display a nihilistic philosophy?

Arts in Action

Since Dadaism was such an effective artistic means of conveying the worldview message that there is no meaning in the world, consider how you might express your meaningful, Christian worldview through art. Your effort will not be like Dadaism because you will be truly attempting to express something that is real and meaningful.

- Using sculpture, painting, mosaics, or whatever medium of art you prefer, create an artwork with a title which expresses a Christian worldview. You may choose to do a Biblical scene, a historical scene, a nature scene, or something from your life. Remember, the point is to try to communicate your worldview through this art.

Architecture

"… OOPS!! …"

For this unit, there is no architecture activity, for the simple reason that during the first world war, everyone was too busy blowing things up to design new buildings!

BOOM!!

Science

In 1916, Paul Langevin of France, developed an underwater ultrasonic source for submarine detection. Though "sonar" (an acronym of SOund NAvigation and Ranging) was not available to the Allies in WWI, it was secretly brought up to full functioning capability during the interim years and used successfully during WWII.

Active sonar sends out an underwater pulse of sound or "ping." When it hits something, it echoes the sound back. This allows the sonar operator to determine how far away the object is, since sound carries through salt water at a constant rate of approximately 4,800 feet per second. If it took two seconds to hear the echoing "ping," the echo traveled 4,800 feet to get to the object and 4,800 feet to get back. WOW!

Do this series of three "experiments" to learn more about underwater sonar:

- First, observe what a sound wave looks like! Using a Slinky, have one person hold one end while you hold the other end across a table. Stretch it loosely, then jerk your end toward your friend. Watch what happens. The motion you see is similar to a sound wave. If you don't have a slinky, you can use a long rope on a sidewalk. The shape of the waves your rope makes is just like the shape of sound waves. Have a friend hold one end while you make short, sweeping motions with your end of the rope. Remember, watch the waves!

- Next, learn about the way sound travels though water. In a swimming pool, have a friend listen to you make a sound while you are both underwater. Then make the same sound above water. Does being underwater make the sound louder and clearer? An optional way to try this experiment is to take two rocks with you into the bathtub. When your ears and hands are submerged under the water, try clicking the rocks together. Next, try clicking the rocks together when both your ears and hands are above the water. Which medium - air or water - allowed the sound to travel more loudly and clearly? Sound waves actually travel through the water more than four times faster than through the air!

- Finally, learn more about echoes. Cliffs or city walls are ideal for this experiment, but you may also want to try it in a large, empty gym or auditorium. Shout a word or message (when it is relatively quiet around you). Then count the number of seconds it takes before you hear an echo. Divide the seconds by two, then by five to get the distance to the cliffs in miles. (Divide by two because the sound traveled twice - to the cliffs and then back to your ears. Divide by five because sound travels one-fifth of a mile per second in air.) You need to be at least forty feet away in order for your ears to have time to hear the echo.

- If you want to play a game about echoes and ultrasound, look for the book, **Make it Work! Sound**, by Alexandra Parsons.

After trying these experiments, look up "sonar" in the encyclopedia or science book. Do you understand the principles used in sonar? How would you explain these principles to young children?

Music

The music of Ralph Vaughn Williams and Gustav Holst stands in stark contrast to the art of the Dadaists. Though they were English composers of the early twentieth century, their style reflects a different use of music than Stravinsky and other expressionistic composers. It was very serious, technically very professional, artful and beautiful, but it was something the average concert-goer could enjoy without feeling assaulted musically. The music of Vaughn Williams and Gustav Holst gained its strength by incorporating and sometimes imitating the music of the common people. In other words, they sometimes put the actual folk tunes in their compositions, but their compositions weren't sing-a-longs - they were truly serious pieces of concert music. Vaughn Williams said, "The composer must not shut himself up and think about art, he must live with his fellows and make his art an expression of the whole life of the community."

- Listen to Holst's "The Planets." Read the program notes that accompany the recording. Consider what Holst writes about the character of each planet and decide whether he conveyed that character in the section he composed for it. How would you describe this music? Do you agree that the music, though very technically demanding, is enjoyable to the average listener? (By the way, listen to this composition, then listen to the sound track composed by John Williams for the movie, **Star Wars**. Do you notice any themes or musical ideas that Williams borrowed from Holst?)

- Listen to Holst's "Suite in F" or "Suite in E-flat" written for band to hear how he incorporated folk songs into his compositions.

- For further study in this time period, find songs from WWI that were sung by the soldiers from your country, or from other countries, as well.

Cooking

During this unit we have learned more about Russia and the Bolshevik Revolution. This is a simple recipe you can make which comes from Russia. It is wonderful on a cold winter's day!

Braised Cucumbers with Dill and Sour Cream

6 small cucumbers, peeled
Salt
6 Tbsp. butter
1 onion, minced

1/4 cup sour cream
2 Tbsp. fresh dill, chopped
Pepper
Pinch of nutmeg

Halve the cucumbers lengthwise and scrape out the seeds. Cut into 2-inch strips. Sprinkle the cucumbers with salt and let stand for 20 minutes. Drain and pat dry. Melt 4 Tbsp. of butter in a saucepan. Add the cucumbers, cover, and cook over low heat until tender, about 10 minutes. In a separate saucepan, melt the remaining butter and sauté the onion for 5 minutes. Remove from the heat and stir in the sour cream and dill. Season with spices. Stir in the cucumbers, heat through, and serve.

Idea Time

Creative Writing

- You are an ace reporter for the "Blow-by-Blow War Report." The use of the newly invented airplane has everyone in suspense - is it strictly for observation, or might it be used as an aggressive military weapon? Uncover the facts and tell the story!

- You belong to one of the Arab tribes which has come to fight the Turks and Germans with Lawrence of Arabia. Write a letter home to your family describing this extremely unusual British soldier. Remember, your family would greatly benefit from hearing something amusing at this point. (You may write in English.)

- Write a want ad on behalf of the German Empire to attract sailors for the new submarines. Since this is a fairly unknown kind of vessel, which stays underwater for LONG periods of time, you are going to have to really use some creative, persuasive techniques. Go for it!

- Write an epic poem about the fall of the Russian monarchy during the Russian Revolution.

- Finish this limerick:

There once was a Kaiser named Bill,
Who thought, "Bigger , yet bigger still"...

  ## Art

- Draw a political cartoon of how necessity was the mother of invention when it came to the tank in WWI.

Drama

- Through the use of drama, show how Vladimir Lenin came to power in Russia during the Bolshevik Revolution. Remember, he was in exile in Switzerland and came back home on a train through the "good graces" of the Germans who were at war with Russia!

The Big Picture

- WWI was a complex, devastating tragedy for millions of people around the world. Through a series of vignettes (either drama or speech), explain to family, friends and neighbors the multi-faceted issues and events of WWI.

Unit Seven

The Rise of Fascism, Nazism, & The Struggle For Independence

Campaign Poster for Hitler/Von Hindenburg

Unit Objectives:

- To learn about fascism and Nazism, why they became popular, and how they differed from communism and democracy;

- to study the beginnings of the Third Reich under Adolf Hitler, and how his anti-Semitism influenced Germany and the Jews;

- to know how the Balfour Declaration of 1917 affected the Jews of Europe and the Middle East;

- to read about the movements for independence and sovereignty of the people in Turkey, India, Ireland, Poland and China;

- to see how the life of Eric Liddell (**Chariots of Fire**) impacted the world for Christ.

Meet the People & Study the Countries:

Here are some people you might meet in this unit:

In the Church:
Eric Liddell   J. Gresham Machen   Isobel Kuhn
Cameron Townsend

In the World:
Adolf Hitler   Benito Mussolini   Kemal Ataturk
Gandhi   Jawaharlal Nehru   Eamon De Valera
Albert Einstein   Sun Yat-sen

You might wish to study one of these countries in depth during this unit:
Italy   India   Turkey
Ireland   China

- **The Holy Bible**
  Proverbs 8:13, 16:18; Zechariah 2:8; Romans 10:14-15; Acts 17:26-27

- **The Rise and Fall of Adolf Hitler** - A World Landmark Book, by William L. Shirer
  The author, William Shirer, also authored **The Rise and Fall of the Third Reich**, which is one
  of the pre-eminent books about Nazi Germany. He has scaled down the level of difficulty for
  this children's biography, and has succeeded magnificently in portraying one of the scariest
  people in world history. Highly recommended!   **Upper elem & up**

- **Hitler** by Albert Marrin
  Described as "the most fascinating and frightening man in history," Hitler's story is told in this
  excellent biography.   **Upper elem & up**

- **Hitler and the Germans** - A Cambridge Topic Book, by Ronald Gray
  This rise of Nazism in Germany is one of the main topics of this book. It shows the
  development of this nationalistic trend, and the atrocities which resulted from it. WWII only
  makes sense as we understand the philosophies undergirding and supporting the Nazi
  mentality.   **Junior High & up**

- **Adolf Hitler** - World Leaders Past & Present, by Dennis Wepman
  An excellent, concise biography of Hitler, this book also includes photos of his life and rule.
  Very interesting!   **Junior High & up**

- **Paul von Hindenburg** - World Leaders Past & Present, by Russell A. Berman
  The legendary German general of WWI, Hindenburg was twice elected president of the
  Weimar Republic. He appointed Hitler to be Chancellor of Germany in 1933, which allowed
  Hitler to take over when Hindenburg died. This excellent book is not only a biography, but it
  also shows the state of affairs in Germany between the two world wars.
                                                                     Junior High & up

- **Albert Einstein** by Elma Ehrlich Levinger
  This is a very readable, extremely interesting biography of one of the greatest physicists of history. Einstein was a German-born Jew who helped Chaim Weizmann raise money for the Hebrew University in Palestine (though he was not a practicing Jew), who supported pacifism until Hitler went to war, and who wrote a letter to President Roosevelt suggesting that the U.S. start a program to build the atomic bomb. Did you know that Einstein was on the Nazi's "hit list"? Fascinating!   **Upper elem & up**

- **Kemal Ataturk** - World Leaders Past & Present, by Frank Tachau
  If you've ever wondered what happened to the Ottoman Empire, and how modern day Turkey emerged at the end of WWI, this book is for you! Ataturk (which means "Father of the Turks") was the Turkish soldier who held back the Allies during their disastrous attempt to take the Gallipoli peninsula in WWI. (Winston Churchill was the British politician who had ordered the attack!) He rose in prominence, eventually becoming a dictator, in order to pull his nation up into the twentieth century.   **Junior High & up**

- **Turkey** - Cultures of the World Series, by Sean Sheehan
  This series of books gives a brief overview of the country's history, its geography, and culture. It is an excellent "primer" for discovering more about modern day Turkey and the Turkish people - and the impact of Ataturk on Turkey.   **Mid elem & up**

- **Turkey** - Life World Library Series, by Desmond Stewart
  Turkey was the heart of the Ottoman Empire. When the empire crumbled after WWI, Turkey emerged as a nation under Ataturk. This excellent overview of Turkey's history will help you put the pieces together. Wonderful photos!   **High school & up**

- **Gandhi and the Struggle for India's Independence** - A Cambridge Topic Book
  by F.W. Rawding
  This is an interesting, well-written look at Gandhi, appropriate for children.
                                                                          Upper elem & up

- **Gandhi** - World Leaders Past & Present, by Catherine Bush
  This is a biography of the man who helped end British rule in India through the use of passive resistance. It is astonishing to consider how effective this method was in demonstrating to the British that they could no longer administrate this part of the Empire. Though violence between different religious groups did accompany the birth of independence in India, the process of attaining independence was remarkably free of violence.
                                                                          Junior High & up

- **Jawaharlal Nehru** - World Leaders Past & Present, by Lila Finck and John P. Hayes
  A fascinating look at India's first prime minister and one of the prime movers in India's bid for independence, this biography also shows how Nehru ably functioned as a world statesman on India's behalf. Highly recommended!   **Junior High & up**

- **Eamon De Valera** - World Leaders Past & Present, by Desmond MacNamara
  Eamon De Valera was one of the most significant leaders in Ireland's struggle for

independence from England. This excellent book allowed me for the first time to understand the complex issues as well as the different factions in Ireland, and why the struggle has continued. Highly recommended!   **Junior High & up**

- **Ireland, A Divided Country** by John Lewis
  The situation in Ireland must be understood in the light of history, or else it is incomprehensible. This book gives a very brief overview of both the history of Ireland and the continuing problems it faces. It is an excellent primer of the troubles.   **Upper elem & up**

- **The Republic of Ireland** - Enchantment of the World Series, by Dennis B. Fradin
  This book is one of the best for giving children an overview of the history, geography, and people of Ireland. It includes the cities, the culture, the work of the people, famous Irish personalities and more. Highly recommended!   **Upper elem & up**

- **The Wearing of the Green - The Irish Rebellion (1916-21)** by Clifford Lindsey Alderman
  A very readable version of the Irish struggle for independence from Great Britain. It ends with a brief description of the state of affairs in 1972.   **Junior High & up**

- **Italy** - Discovering our Heritage Series, by Anthony DiFranco
  This series of books looks at the history, geography, and culture of a country. There is a brief description of Mussolini and fascism, and of what happened to Italy after WWII.
                                                                Mid elem & up

- **Italy** - Enchantment of the World Series, by R. Conrad Stein
  This series of books gives a brief overview of the country's history, its geography, and culture. An excellent "primer" for discovering more about Italy and the Italian people. Learn about Garibaldi, Mussolini, fascism, and more.   **Mid elem & up**

- **Poland** - Cultures of the World Series, by Jay Heale
  Poland has a rich history and culture, but has often been the unwilling property of a foreign master. Learn more about this country and its history - including the freedom won after WWI and Hitler's invasion which started WWII.   **Mid elem & up**

- **Poland** - Festivals of the World, by Aldona Maria Zwierzynska-Coldicott
  A fun look at some of the holidays of Poland including a recipe for Nut Mazurek.
                                                                Mid elem & up

- **The Man who Changed China - The Story of Sun Yat-sen** - A World Landmark Book
  by Pearl Buck
  If you have ever wondered how China went from the Boxer Rebellion to the Communist Revolution, this book will provide a tremendous understanding. Sun Yat-sen spent almost his entire life trying to bring a democratic form of government to his beloved China by revolutionary means through the overthrow of the Manchu Dynasty. Highly recommended!
                                                                Upper elem & up

- **Sun Yat-Sen** - World Leaders Past & Present, by Jeffrey Barlow
  To understand modern China, one must understand what happened after the Manchu

Dynasty. Sun Yat-Sen was a major factor in helping the country move from this imperial government to a government more representative of the people. This book shows the transition, and why he is known as the "Father of the Country." **Junior High & up**

- **Eric Liddell** - Christian Heroes Then & Now, by Janet & Geoff Benge
  Wonderfully written, this series of Christian biographies is fascinating, factual, and historically accurate. Eric Liddell is one of my heroes, and this book does an excellent job of conveying his life and the faithfulness of his Lord. Highly recommended! **Mid elem & up**

- **Eric Liddell** - Men of Faith Series, by Catherine Swift
  Subtitled, "The Scottish hero of the 1924 Paris Olympics whose story was portrayed in **Chariots of Fire**," this is the faith-building story of a man used by God on the athletic field and on the mission field. Highly recommended! **Upper elem & up**

- **The Flying Scotsman** by Sally Magnusson
  The author writes, "Who was this man, Eric Liddell? What kind of person was it who could compete so effectively, yet turn down the chance of Olympic glory so effortlessly... who could shrug off all the super-star adulation and head for China as casually as if he were popping off for a week-end in London... above all, who had such a shattering impact on all who met him that nobody, nobody at all, ever had a bad word to say of him?" Another excellent biography of Eric Liddell, this may be more readily available at the library. Highly recommended!
  Upper elem & up

- **Athens to Atlanta - 100 Years of Glory** by Lee Benson, Doug Robinson, Dee Benson
  A look at the Olympics from 1896 to 1996, this coffee table book contains the 1924 Paris Olympics where Eric Liddell competed, as well as the 1936 Berlin Olympics where Jesse Owens (an African-American competitor) completely ruined Hitler's plans for showing the superiority of the Aryan race! **Upper elem & up**

- **Isobel Kuhn** - Women of Faith Series, by Lois Hoadley Dick
  This is the biography of a Canadian woman who was called to the Lisu people of China in the late 1920's. If you wonder what life was like for Chinese Christians when the Communists took over China, this story will make it clear. Highly recommended! **Upper elem & up**

- **1930's - Take Ten Years** by Ken Hills
  A year by year look at the decade of the 1930's, this book is set up with a newspaper appearance. **Upper elem & up**

- **Dates with Destiny - The 100 Most Important Dates in Church History**
  by A. Kenneth Curtis, J. Stephen Lang, and Randy Petersen
  Beginning with the year 64 in Rome and continuing to 1976, this book is filled with short descriptions of events and people within the Church. For this chapter read about the first Christian radio broadcast, and Cameron Townsend with the Summer Institute of Linguistics. Highly recommended! **Upper elem & up**

- **From Jerusalem to Irian Jaya - A Biographical History of Christian Missions**
  by Ruth A. Tucker

This is the best book on the history of world missions available. Included are short biographies of missionaries all over the world, categorized by their geographical area of service. I consider this an indispensable resource for the study of **World Empires, World Missions, World Wars**. For this chapter read pages 421-425. Highly recommended!

Upper elem & up

- **The Unpleasantness at the Bellona Club** by Dorothy Sayers
  Dorothy Sayers was one of the great mystery writers of the twentieth century. This classic is one of our favorites because of the unexpectedly happy conclusion. **Junior High & up**

- **Video: Chariots of Fire**
  This is the incredible story of Eric Liddell and his Christian witness at the 1924 Paris Olympics.
  For the whole family!

Talk Together

Albert Einstein

- Listen to **What in the World's Going On Here?, Volume Two**, Tape One. What was the most interesting aspect to you of this time period between the two world wars? Why? What other questions about this time period would you like to have answered?
  History Journal: Write those questions down and, as you study more material, write the answers to your questions. Also, write short bios of the people you study whom you find interesting. Illustrate the bios.

- Why do you think the 1929 Wall Street Stock Market Crash had such a devastating impact on America? - On Europe? - On Germany? Do you think the crash was a surprise? Why or why not?

- Imagine you were living in Germany in the early 1930's. Superinflation has hit your economy. Do you think you would be interested in listening to a man who promises a solution? Why or why not? What was Hitler's solution?

- How would you explain the difference between a healthy pride in your own nation and the unhealthy pride of fascism? Where does one draw the line between healthy and unhealthy pride? How does racism fit in with fascism? Do you see evidences today of fascism or racism? What might be the potential outcome of this?

- How does Darwinian evolution fit into the idea of fascism? What do you think "the survival of the fittest" has to do with people and nations? Do you think this a right idea or a wrong idea? Why?

- Why do you think Hitler blamed all of Germany's problems on the Jews? Why do you think many Germans were ready to listen to this? Do you see any similarities anywhere in the world today? What is the potential outcome of this kind of blame and hatred?

- Do you think Hitler was a popular politician with the common people in Germany in the early 1930's? Why or why not? Do you think he was popular with the aristocrats? Why or why not? Do you think he was popular with the current government? Why or why not?

- Do you think the Nazi Blood Purge should have been a "wake-up call" to the Germans and the rest of Europe? Why do you think the European leaders chose to ignore Hitler's atrocities prior to WWII? Do you see any similarities in the world today?

- Many historians have indicated that Hitler could have been stopped if his violations of the Treaty of Versailles had been punished. Do you agree with this point of view? Why or why not? Consider this: What happens to a child who does something wrong and no one corrects him?

- The Spanish Civil War set the elected government (communist) against the fascists. Do you think the elected government would have been able to stay in power if the fascists had not been helped by Germany and Italy? Why or why not? How was this war a "practice run" for WWII? How do you think this war might have helped German pilots, soldiers and military tacticians?

- Why do you think Japan preferred an alliance to Germany and Italy, rather than to other European countries? How did the fascism of Italy and the Nazism of Germany compare to the Japanese military attitude?

- Why do you think Winston Churchill believed that there would be war, while Neville Chamberlain believed there would be peace? What do you think might have happened if Neville Chamberlain had listened to Churchill?

- Do you believe it was a providential act of God that began opening a homeland for the Jews in Palestine? Why or why not? How might this have affected the German Jews after Hitler began his anti-Semitic push? Do you think life in Palestine during this time period was easy? Why or why not? How do you think the Arabs in Palestine viewed the increasing numbers of Jewish immigrants to Palestine?

- Why do you think Hitler wanted the chancellor of Austria to resign? What propaganda value do you think there was in having the new (Nazi) Austrian chancellor ask Hitler to come to Austria?

- Describe the Munich Agreement of 1938. Does it seem unnatural to you that the leader of the country under discussion was not invited to this conference? Why do you think Neville Chamberlain proclaimed, "Peace in our time," after this conference?

- Why do you think Hitler waited until March to take the rest of Czechoslovakia? (Hint: Consider the time of year.) What affect did this action have upon the rest of Europe?

- Hitler signed a non-aggression pact with the Soviet Union in August, 1939. Why? How would it benefit Germany? How would it benefit the Soviet Union? Did Hitler keep his word? How was Poland affected by this pact? What do you think caused Chamberlain to threaten war with Germany if Hitler took Poland?

- What do you think was Hitler's goal? Why? If he had succeeded, how do you think your life would be different today?

- Why did Eric Liddell refuse to run the 100 meter race at the 1924 Olympics in Paris? What do you think about his decision? How would this apply to your life? Do you hold the same convictions as Eric Liddell? Why or why not?

Teaching Time!

Seminar Outline

I. Conditions Between the World Wars
   A. Stock Market Crash on Wall Street - 1929
      1. America enters Great Depression
   B. Worldwide impact of Stock Market Crash
      1. Hardest on Germans
         a. Still paying off fines from WWI
         b. Superinflation
         c. Savings are wiped out overnight
         d. One man offers solution - Adolph Hitler

II. Fascism and Nazism
   A. Fascism
      1. Opposes communism
      2. Based on national pride
      3. Racism
      4. Based on evolutionary concept of the survival of the fittest
      5. Fascist Ruler in Italy - Mussolini
      6. Fascist Ruler in Germany - Hitler
   B. Beginnings of Nazism
      1. Hitler joined workers group - 7th member
      2. Renamed it the NAZI party
      3. Blamed everything on the Jews
      4. Brownshirts (S.A.)
         a. Terror tactics
         b. Destroy opponents
      5. Hitler became Chancellor - 1933
         a. Eliminated all other parties
         b. "Nazified" the entire political structure
III. The Third Reich
   A. Hitler became Fuehrer - 1934
      1. Ordered "Nazi Blood Purge"
      2. Sets up The Third Reich
   B. Kristallnacht (night of broken glass) - 1938
      1. Jewish businesses and synagogues burned or destroyed
      2. More than 30,000 Jews arrested and sent to prison camps
   C. Hitler violates Versailles Treaty Terms
      1. Rearms
         a. Builds German tanks (Panzers)
         b. German air force (Luftwaffe)
         c. Submarines
      2. Sends troops into the Rhineland - 1936

IV. Spanish Civil War - 1936
    A. Practice for the Germans and Italians
    B. "Republican" government
        1. Elected communist/socialist government
        2. Opposes Catholic Church
    C. "Nationalists"
        1. Fascists
        2. Army
        3. Supports Catholic Church
        4. Helped by Italy and Germany
    D. Lasts until 1939
        1. Franco
            a. Nationalist
            b. Takes power (to 1975)
    E. Spain stays neutral in WWII

V. Selecting sides
    A. Axis Powers
        1. Germany
        2. Italy
        3. Japan (very militaristic in the Pacific)
    B. England
        1. Prime Minister Neville Chamberlain wants peace
        2. Winston Churchill says that there will be war

VI. Israel and the Middle East
    A. Balfour Declaration of 1917
    B. England took control of Egypt in 1882
        1. Protect their interest in the Middle East - the Suez Canal
        2. Protect their trade with India; trade with the far East
    C. After WWI, England and France were "protecting" the Middle East
    D. Calls for a Jewish state, the birth of Zionism - Beginning in 1896
        1. Theodore Herzl
        2. First Settlement in Palestine by European Jews - 1909
        3. Hebrew being spoken again
        4. Desert began to bloom under the technology and skill of the Jews
        5. Arab neighbors became increasingly concerned
    E. Hitler showed his anti-Semitism
        1. Many German Jews fled to Palestine
        2. Others fled to nearby European countries

VII. Escalation to WWII
    A. Hitler tells the chancellor of Austria to resign - February 1938
    B. Hitler marches his troops into Austria - March 1938
    C. Munich Agreement - September 1938
    D. Hitler takes the rest of Czechoslovakia - March 1939
    E. Hitler signs a nonaggression pact with Soviet Union - August 1939
    F. Chamberlain tells Hitler that if he takes Poland, England will go to war

Timeline

On your timeline, mark Adolph Hitler, Benito Mussolini, the Spanish Civil War, Kristallnacht, Gandhi, Albert Einstein, Sun Yat-sen, Ataturk, Eamon De Valera, Winston Churchill, Neville Chamberlain, Eric Liddell, Isobel Kuhn, Balfour Declaration, Munich Agreement.

Research & Reporting

- Find one of the books listed at the beginning of this unit, along with the encyclopedia or other history resource book, for basic information on fascism. Write a report detailing the essential components and historical outworkings of this political philosophy.

- Research and report on the life and government of Adolf Hitler. Include details of his childhood, military experience during World War One, and his belief in Aryan supremacy.

- Research and report on anti-Semitism. Show the major areas of the world that have encouraged persecution of the Jews and the major periods of time when this persecution has been on a large scale.

- The Balfour Declaration of 1917 declared that "His Majesty's Government view with favour the establishment in Palestine of a national home for the Jewish people, and will use their best endeavors to facilitate the achievement of this object, it being clearly understood that nothing shall be done which may prejudice the civil and religious rights of existing non-Jewish communities in Palestine or the rights and political status enjoyed by Jews in any other country." Research and report on the Zionist movement begun in the late 1800's, Chaim Weizmann - whose scientific work for Great Britain aided tremendously in the Allied effort during WWI and the effect of the Balfour Declaration on Palestine.

- Study the life and scientific theories developed by Albert Einstein. Write a report about what you discover.

- Research and report on the rise of Turkey as a modern nation from the ashes of the Ottoman Empire. Describe the life, philosophy, and work of Kemal Ataturk who was known as the "Father of Turkey."

- Study and write about how and why Ireland was divided into two countries, showing how this continues to impact the stability of Northern Ireland. Include the Easter Uprising and Eamon De Valera.

- Italy became a united kingdom in 1861. Research and report on how it changed from a monarchy-based government to a fascist dictator, including a brief description of Benito Mussolini.

- Study and describe the changes in China after the fall of the Manchu Dynasty. Report on the life of Sun Yat-sen, and how his many failures contributed to the significant changes in China.

- Eric Liddell was a true Christian hero - not just for his stand at the 1924 Olympics, but also in how he lived his life. Write a research paper describing his childhood, his education, his athletics, and his missionary service in China.

- Jessie Owens was an American athlete who participated in the 1936 Olympics in Berlin. Research and report on his life and the effect his Olympic victory had upon Hitler's philosophy of Aryan supremacy.

- Study and write about Isobel Kuhn, the Canadian woman who became a missionary to the Lisu people of China. Include a description of the way life changed when the communists began to take over this area.

- Research and report on the country of Czechoslovakia and the Munich Agreement. Include a description of the Sudentenland and why this was important to Hitler's plans. Describe Chamberlain and Dadier's participation in the Munich Agreement, contrasting it with Churchill's pronouncement of doom.

- Research and report on the country of Poland. Show how it became independent after World War One, and why both Germany and Russia considered it such a desirable piece of real estate.

Brain Stretchers

- Compare and contrast fascism and Nazism with communism; with democracy. How are they different? How are they the same? Show what life is like for the common person under each of these regimes.

- Research and report on how Einstein's theory of relativity in the sciences was wrongly applied to philosophy. Show how the absolute standards of right and wrong were considered no longer applicable due to this theory, and explain what Einstein believed about this misapplication.

- Research and report on the life and philosophy of Mahatma Gandhi, and how this affected the British Empire in India. Show the areas where Gandhi's form of protest was effective, and where it was not. (Hint: How did the major competing religions of India work out their differences?) Though he is revered in India, what was the lasting effect of his life (apart from the ending of British rule)?

- Compare and contrast the Nationalist Party of China with the Communist Party. Show why they worked together at times, why they fought at other times, who was their common enemy, and the effect upon China of this struggle between the two factions.

Vocabulary

fascism	Nazism	Reich	anti-Semitism
sovereignty	chancellor	dictator	independence
nationalistic	pacifist	passive	factions
superinflation	purge	atrocities	violation
nonaggression	terrorist	Zionism	Aryan

In this unit there is a great emphasis on the political events and philosophies between the world wars.

- Your assignment is to collect as many political terms as you find in this unit's study, and define them.

Hands On!

**Maps
and
Mapping**

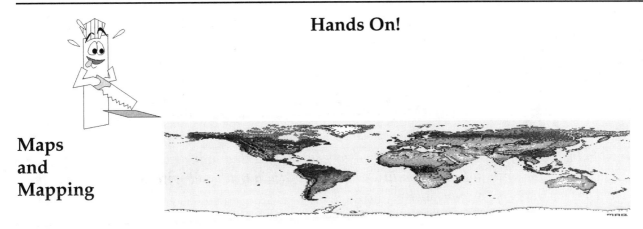

- Using an atlas, encyclopedia, or other resource locate Germany, Italy, Spain, Palestine, Turkey, India, Ireland, Poland, and China.

- What are the names of the cities and countries that today occupy the same area? What is the capital city, religion, population, major export, and type of government in each modern country? What is the status of Christianity in these countries?

- On a clean worksheet map, shade with various colors the areas of the world which gained independence during this time. Also, identify the areas of the world which were being taken over by fascism and/or Nazism.

- Consult a relief map to discover the terrain found in Spain. Are there deserts, forest, mountains, islands? Label them. What kind of climate is typical in each of the different terrains? How did these different terrains and climates affect the Spanish Civil War?

- Consult a relief map to discover the terrain found in any of the countries which gained independence during this time period (Turkey, India, Ireland, Poland, China). Are there deserts, forest, mountains, islands? Label them. What kind of climate is typical in each of the different terrains? How did these different terrains and climates affect the struggle for independence?

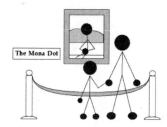

The Mona Dot

Art Appreciation

In contrast to the Dadaist artists/philosophers who gave up on meaning in life and art, there were humanist artists in the early twentieth century who tried to attain truth and spiritual reality through style known as "abstract" or "neo-plasticism" art.

Piet Mondrian, a Dutch painter, first created this style of painting through contact with a former Catholic priest turned theosophist, H. Schoenmaekers. This man believed this his "plastic mathematics" would allow one to "penetrate, by contemplation, the hidden construction of reality." It was his stress on the use of geometric forms and primary colors which gave Mondrian a way of painting a picture that had "spiritual significance" without any visible connecting link to nature or the world. That is what made abstract art different from just painting a pattern or piece of decoration - it had "meaning" behind it! (Though just who might understand this meaning is a bit of a mystery...) This style of painting was intended to be the wake-up call to a messed up world. Mondrian, in writing about this art form, stated, "In the vital reality of the abstract, the new man has outgrown the sentiments of nostalgia, joy, rapture, sadness, horror, etc: in the emotion made constant by beauty, these are rendered pure and clarified."

*H. R. Rookmaaker, in **Modern Art and the Death of a Culture**, writes, "The work of these painters could perhaps be explained by saying that Mondrian and the others were building a beautiful fortress for spiritual humanity, very rational, very formal: but they did so on the very edge of a deep, deep abyss, one into which they did not dare to look."*

Without God, man can not find true spirituality though he hopes it is there. Abstract art shows us clearly the truth of Romans 1:21-22.

- Look in the encyclopedia under "Painting" to see an abstract painting by Mondrian. How would you describe this painting? Does it convey the meaning Mondrian expressed in the paragraph above? Why or why not? H. Rookmaaker wrote that Mondrian, in a way, "defined twentieth-century style." Consider his painting and answer the question of how you think Mondrian had a major influence on modern art - in what ways are other works of art or architecture reflecting the influence of abstract art?

Arts in Action

Have you seen the "salvation bracelet" with the different colored beads representing various aspects of he Gospel message? The color black stands for sin, red for the blood of Christ, white for redeemed souls, green for growth in Christ, and yellow for heaven.

- Rather than creating abstract art which no one understands, we want to take the idea of using colors and lines to tell the story which everyone needs to understand! Try this: Create a booklet, poster or painting which tells the Gospel story using simple forms and the colors named above. You may want to use a cross, a fish, a cup, bread, or other Christian symbols. Remember that your purpose is to communicate a spiritual message of Biblical truth to your audience through a method similar to Mondrian's use of basic colors and simple forms.

" ... OOPS!! ..."

Architecture

*The Bauhaus school of design was among the most significant architectural groups of the twentieth century. Michael Raeburn, in **An Outline of World Architecture** states, "...the Bauhaus was of incalculable influence in twentieth-century architecture and design... (The philosophy was that buildings) should be designed with the utmost simplicity and solely with its practical function in mind...the most functional is the most beautiful." This style of architecture showed a complete break with the past, with historical styles and traditions, making it one of the significant movements in modern architecture.*

- In the encyclopedia, look up "Architecture," "Gropius, Walter," and "Bauhaus" to see examples of this style of architecture and design. How would you describe this style? How is it similar to Frank Lloyd Wright's designs? How is it different from the architecture of the 1800's? How is it different from all of the other architecture in history?

Science

In 1928, a revolutionary discovery was made by Alexander Fleming that would eventually save so many lives that it seemed almost miraculous. Where was this discovery made? In a moldy dish! Penicillin, the first of the antibiotic medicines, was at first glance an unlikely miracle drug, since it looked like a simple mold. However, when Alexander Fleming, a medical researcher, carefully examined the dish with this mold, he saw that it had killed all of the deadly bacteria he was trying to grow, or "culture," for medical research purposes. With careful observation and experimentation, he discovered that this mold would kill all the common deadly bacteria such as staphylococci, streptococci, pneumococci, and even the bacilli of diphtheria. It took another dozen years to create penicillin in great enough quantities to be medically useful, but this amazing breakthrough in medicine was worth waiting for.

- Create your own mold! Using an aluminum pan at least two inches deep and six inches square, fill the pan with about one inch of soil or compost. On top of the soil, add a layer of orange peels and old bread. Lightly water this layer. Cover the pan with plastic wrap, sealing it tightly with a large rubber band. Place the pan in a warm, dark place for a day or two. Check to see if the mold is growing. If not, add a bit more water and try it again. Be sure to carefully handle the disposal of the soil and mold after the successful completion of your experiment. This would be great "stuff" to add to your compost pile!

 # Music

Aaron Copland and George Gershwin, two American composers, continued the line of technically profound and musically serious compositions, but they again made music that was approachable to the common people of the day, incorporating that home-grown phenomenon known as jazz music. American jazz was utilized by these composers in the 1920's, while cowboy folk songs (songs of the American West), Cuban, and Mexican music provided thematic material in the 1930's.

Gershwin desired to bridge the gap between entertainment and serious music. Some of the tunes people consider his most famous songs were written for Broadway musicals, and yet, one of the most popular symphonic pieces performed around the world is his **Rhapsody in Blue**.

- Listen to Gershwin's **Rhapsody in Blue**. How would you describe this music? Do you hear how he appealed to simpler musical tastes, such as dance music or sing-a-long style, but was able to set them into serious professional compositions? How would you compare this with other compositions by composers like Tchaikovsky or Holst? You may also want to listen to Gershwin's opera, **Porgy and Bess**.

- Listen to Copland's **Fanfare for the Common Man**. Do you recognize this piece of music? How would you describe it? How would you compare this with other compositions by composers like Tchaikovsky or Holst? You may also want to listen to Copland's ballet, **Rodeo**.

- For further study in this time period, you might enjoy swing style music. Listen to Glenn Miller or Benny Goodman recordings for a flavor of this style.

Cooking

In this unit, we have had the opportunity to study more about India and its struggle for independence. What a wonderful excuse to try my favorite food!

Chicken Curry

Authentic curry recipes will instruct you to make your own curry powder from a number of spices. Try it sometime! Generally, we just use a good curry powder from the grocery store.

1 Tbsp. butter	3/4 tsp. salt
1 cup finely chopped, pared apple	2 to 3 tsp. curry powder
1 cup sliced celery	3/4 cup cold chicken broth
1/2 cup chopped onion	2 cups milk
1 clove garlic, minced	2 cups diced cooked chicken (or turkey)
2 Tbsp. cornstarch	

In a large frypan, melt butter. Add apple, celery, onion, and garlic. Cook till onion is tender. Combine cornstarch, curry, salt and broth in a bowl, whisking until smooth. Stir into onion mixture, add milk. Cook and stir until mixture thickens. Stir in chicken and heat through. Serve over hot rice, and offer any combination of these condiments: Mango chutney, coconut, raisins, chopped peanuts, chopped green onions, chopped hard-boiled eggs, bananas.

Idea Time

Creative Writing

- You have the extreme honor of interviewing the great German general and current president of the Weimar Republic, Paul von Hindenburg. He has just appointed a new Chancellor for Germany, one Adolph Hitler. Find out for the readers of your magazine, "The Republic Reporter," just who this new Chancellor is and why von Hindenburg appointed him. Be sure to include the President's view on the future.

- As a British soldier stationed in India, write a letter home to your folks describing the new "passive resistance" movement being headed up by a lawyer named Gandhi. Describe your personal experience with this effective technique in the bid for Indian independence.

- Write a short story for children about Isobel Kuhn, a missionary in the late 1920's to the Lisu ("dirt") people of China.

- For your highly controversial television news program, "Time is Short," interview Winston Churchill for his perspective on Hitler and on Neville Chamberlain. Why does Churchill believe there will be war?

- Write an epic poem about the tragedy of Kristallnacht.

Art

- Draw a political cartoon showing superinflation in Germany with the corresponding popularity of Hitler's anti-Semitic, anti-Weimar, anti-Treaty of Versailles appeal. The point of your cartoon is to ask whether the revenge sought at the Treaty of Versailles was worth the price of bringing Hitler to power.

Drama

- Dramatize the life of Eric Liddell. Include his childhood in China, school in Great Britain, Olympics in Paris (with his "awful" running style!), and his work in China.

The Big Picture

- What happens when people listen to someone who promises them personal peace and prosperity, yet asks them to shut their eyes to wrongs being committed against others? Explore what you have learned about this during your study of the interim time between the wars. Use art, drama, short stories, first person accounts, speeches and more to share with family, friends and neighbors.

Unit Eight

World War II & Miraculous Deliverances

An American (Army) in Paris

Unit Objectives:

- To become familiar with:

    - The Phony War
    - The Blitzkrieg
    - The Battle of Britain
    - The Battle of the Atlantic
    - The War in the Pacific
    - The War in North Africa
    - The Normandy Invasion
    - Victory in Europe
    - Victory in the Pacific;

- to discover the miraculous occurrences that changed the course of the war;

- to learn about the concentration camps of Nazi Germany and Corrie ten Boom's story of God's faithfulness inside the camps.

Meet the People & Study the Countries:

Here are some people you might meet in this unit:

In the Church:

Dietrich Bonhoeffer   Corrie ten Boom   Gladys Aylward
Rees Howells

In the World:

Adolf Hitler   Winston Churchill   General Montgomery
General Rommel   Tojo   Douglas MacArthur

You might wish to study one of these places in depth during this unit:

Japan   North Africa   Islands of the Pacific

- **The Holy Bible**
  Psalm 54:1-4, 102:1-13; Proverbs 20:18, 24:6; Ecclesiastes 3:8; Ephesians 6:10-18

- **World War II** - Wars That Changed the World Series, by Ken Hills
  This is an excellent "primer" for children about WWII. It includes all of the major fronts of the war.   **Mid elem & up**

- **The Battle for the Atlantic** - A World Landmark Book, by Jay Williams
  Because England is an island nation, Hitler planned to prevent any supplies bound for England from coming through by the use of his submarines and navy ships, while at the same time bombing the British to bring them to their knees. He was so successful at sea early on, that, in March of 1941, Winston Churchill proclaimed "the Battle of the Atlantic." This book describes in fascinating detail this ongoing battle. Highly recommended!
  Upper elem & up

- **The Sinking of the Bismarck** - A World Landmark Book, by William L. Shirer
  At the moment of England's greatest peril in WWII, when the Nazis had succeeded in destroying many British merchant and naval ships, the most powerful ship in the world was put into German service - the Bismarck. This book details the incredible story of how the British, against all odds, were able to sink her. Highly Recommended! **Upper elem & up**

- **The Miracle of Dunkirk**, by Walter Lord
  As stated on the jacket, "This is the story of the greatest rescue of all time." Winston Churchill called the rescue of 338,000 Allied soldiers from the beaches of Dunkirk, "a miracle of deliverance." Though this is a secular book, it is filled with incidents that can only be explained by the supernatural intervention of God. Highly recommended!
  High School & up

- **The Battle of Britain** - A World Landmark Book, by Quentin Reynolds
  A first person account of the bombing of Britain by Hitler's Germany, this book is a perfect introduction to the "never give in" spirit of the British. Highly recommended!
  Upper elem & up

- **Siege of Leningrad** - World at War Series, by R. Conrad Stein
  This is a fantastic series for children about World War II. The siege of Leningrad is one of the most amazing stories of the war - a city under siege by the Nazis for almost nine hundred days!   **Mid elem & up**

- **Thirty Seconds Over Tokyo** - A World Landmark Book, by Captain Ted W. Lawson
  Written by one of the pilots who dropped bombs on Tokyo shortly after Pearl Harbor, this is a tense accounting of one of the U.S.'s greatest morale-boosters in WWII. Can't-put-it-down suspense!   **Upper elem & up**

- **Midway - Battle for the Pacific** - A World Landmark Book,
  by Captain Edmund L. Castillo, USN
  Landmark books provide remarkable detail in an understandable format. In this title, a blow by blow description of the Battle of Midway - the turning point in the War of the Pacific - is given. Even more importantly, the battle is analyzed, helping the reader to learn why the Japanese, with vastly superior numbers, lost to the U.S. Fascinating! Highly recommended.
  Upper elem & up

- **Miracle at Midway,** by Charles Mercer
  The author served as an intelligence officer in the Pacific during WWII, and this experience brings the "miracle" at Midway to life!   **Junior High & up**

- **Nisei Regiment** - World at War Series, by R. Conrad Stein
  This is a fantastic series for children about World War II. During WWII, a regiment of soldiers was formed, all of whom were Japanese-American. Their accomplishments were astounding!
  Mid elem & up

- **Japan** - Enchantment of the World Series, by Carol Greene
  This series of books gives a brief overview of the country's history, its geography, and culture. An excellent "primer" for discovering more about Japan and the Japanese people. (There is a brief description of the mythological origin of the emperors.) Chapter Five discusses the modern history of Japan, and how WWII impacted Japan.   **Mid elem & up**

- **Hirohito** - World Leaders Past & Present
  This is a biography of the Japanese emperor at the time of WWII. What a fascinating look behind-the-scenes!   **Junior High & up**

- **The Flying Tigers** - A World Landmark Book, by John Toland
  Did you know that the war in the Pacific actually began in 1937? That was when Japan attacked China. This book recounts the incredible story of the American pilots who, by their daring and skill, kept China from being completely overrun. Highly recommended!
  Upper elem & up

- **Fall of Singapore** - World At War Series, by R. Conrad Stein
  This is a fantastic series for children about World War II. The fall of Singapore was the worst defeat in England's history, and also the beginning of the end of European colonial empires in the East. Fascinating!   **Mid elem & up**

- **Guadalcanal Diary** - A World Landmark Book, by Richard Tregaskis
  This was written by a war correspondent who had firsthand experience of the battle for the island of Guadalcanal (one of the Solomon Islands). This battle was one of the turning points of the war in the Pacific. Highly recommended!   **Upper elem & up**

- **Battle of Guadalcanal** - World At War Series, by R. Conrad Stein
  This is a fantastic series for children about World War II. In August of 1942, the American 1st Marine Division attacked this Japanese stronghold in the Solomon Islands. This little book tells for children the story of what happened.   **Mid elem & up**

- **D-Day - The Invasion of Europe** - American Heritage Junior Library, by Al Hine
  This is a blow by blow accounting of one of the most significant events of WWII. The Allies could have been forced back into the sea by the Nazis - this book explains why that did not happen. Highly recommended!   **Upper elem & up**

- **The Story of D-Day** - A World Landmark Book, by Bruce Bliven, Jr.
  Subtitled, "The battle that turned the tide of World War II," this book shows the intense drama of D-Day from an eye-witness account, photos, and factual information about the equipment and methods used to storm the beaches. Highly recommended!   **Mid elem & up**

- **From Pearl Harbor to Okinawa** - A World Landmark Book, by Bruce Bliven Jr.
  Subtitled, "The War in the Pacific - 1941-1945," this, another fantastic Landmark Book, shows the events of the war from the Japanese attack on Pearl Harbor to their surrender after the two atomic bombs were dropped. Highly recommended!   **Mid elem & up**

- **Twenty and Ten** by Claire Huchet Bishop
  The incredible, true story of a French school in WWII under German occupation which decides to hide ten Jewish refugee children. There is also a video of this story entitled, **Miracle at Moreaux.** Highly recommended!   **Great Read Aloud**

- **Sky - A True Story of Resistance During World War II** by Hanneke Ippisch
  Hanneke Ippisch was born in Holland, the daughter of a Protestant minister. In 1945, she was incarcerated for working with a Dutch resistance organization during WWII. This book is the true story of her experiences - and it is truly incredible! Highly recommended!
                Upper elem & up

- **The Seabees of World War II** - A World Landmark Book,
  by Commander Edmund L. Castillo, USN
  Written by the "King Bee" of the seabees, this is an amazing story of people who accomplished unbelievable engineering feats during WWII. The author writes, "Trying to capture the Seabees on paper is a little like trying to describe a wildcat that has the skill of a master mechanic, the tenacity of a bulldog, the speed of lightning, the ingenuity of Thomas Edison, the humor of Bob Hope, and the dedication to duty of John Paul Jones." We couldn't put it down!   **Upper elem & up**

- **The Story of the Paratroops** - A World Landmark Book, by George Weller
  Paratroopers played a remarkable part in WWII. Learn how a Dutch sniper quite possibly saved England by shooting the leader of the German paratroopers at the beginning of the war! Highly recommended! **Upper elem & up**

- **The U.S. Frogmen of World War II** - A World Landmark Book, by Wyatt Blassingame
  The use of divers in war began initially with World War I. It became, however, a vital part of the war in the Pacific during WWII. This book also tells the remarkable story of how six Italians (riding their torpedoes!) sunk three British ships in the port of Alexandria, Egypt - which terminated the British presence in the Mediterranean - without loss of life. Amazing book. **Upper elem & up**

- **Medical Corps Heroes of World War II** - A World Landmark Book, by Wyatt Blassingame
  This is an amazing account of courageous doctors and aids who risked their lives to save others. It will help to "round out" your understanding of the dynamics of World War II. Highly recommended. **Upper elem & up**

- **Combat Nurses of World War II** - A World Landmark Book, by Wyatt Blassingame
  Another group of nurses, in a long line of nurses beginning with Florence Nightingale, who risked their lives to help care for the soldiers wounded in war. This book provides a unique perspective on some of the battles of WWII. Highly recommended. **Upper elem & up**

- **People in History** by R.J. Unstead
  A wonderful series of short biographies, this book begins with the Roman invasion of Britain and continues through WWII. It is written for younger children, though even adults will find it informative! **Elementary & up**

- **Flight of the Fugitives** - Trailblazer Books, by Dave & Neta Jackson
  Historical fiction for children, this is the story of Gladys Aylward and her mission in China before and during WWII. Highly recommended! **Mid elem & up**

- **Gladys Aylward** - Christian Heroes Then and Now, by Janet & Geoff Benge
  Wonderfully written, this series of Christian biographies is fascinating, factual, and historically accurate. Gladys Aylward went to China as a missionary, though she flunked missionary school! Learn more about her, and the way God was able to use this "small woman," in this excellent book. Highly recommended! **Mid elem & up**

- **Gladys Aylward** - Women of Faith Series, by Catherine Swift
  Another biography of this amazing woman who obeyed God's call, this book describes the many incredible adventures of Gladys' life. **Upper elem & up**

- **The Small Woman** by Alan Burgess
  Wonderfully told, this biography of Gladys Aylward also gives an authentic flavor of China before the Communist Revolution. Highly recommended! **Upper elem & up**

- **The Hiding Place** by Corrie ten Boom
  This is the autobiography of an amazing woman who learned to trust God. She and her family aided the Dutch resistance effort and helped to hide Jews in Holland during WWII. The family was caught and sent to a concentration camp. Only Corrie was released - to a worldwide ministry which endured for decades. This book changed my life. Highly recommended!
  Upper elem & up

- **Corrie ten Boom** - Christian Heroes Then and Now, by Janet & Geoff Benge
  Wonderfully written, this series of Christian biographies is fascinating, factual, and historically accurate. Corrie ten Boom's life is a tremendous testimony of God's grace in the midst of overwhelming troubles. Highly recommended!
  Mid elem & up

- **Escape from Warsaw** by Ian Serraillier
  Historical fiction about three children separated from their parents in Warsaw during WWII. They set out to try to find their father in Switzerland with tremendous courage and faith. Excellent!
  Upper elem & up

- **The Story of the Trapp Family Singers** by Maria Augusta Trapp
  This is the story which inspired the movie, **The Sound of Music**. It is very interesting to get a glimpse into the life of a family whose husband and father had fought on the side of the Kaiser in WWI, and now takes his family away from everything they had ever known. (This was a Catholic family, and Catholic theology is described to some degree in the book.)   Fascinating!
  Junior High & up

- **Winston Churchill** - A World Landmark Book, by Quentin Reynolds
  The author writes, "As a war correspondent in London during the worst days of the blitz, I saw what one great human being - namely, Winston Churchill - could do to hold together a nation literally on the verge of being annihilated." This is a fantastic biography, well-written, which gives some of the amazing details of the life of Churchill. Highly recommended!
  Upper elem & up

- **Never Give In** - Leader in Action Series, by Stephen Mansfield
  According to Henry Kissinger, "Our age finds it difficult to come to grips with Churchill. The political leaders with whom we are familiar generally aspire to be superstars rather than heroes. The distinction is crucial. Superstars strive for approbation; heroes walk alone. Superstars crave consensus; heroes define themselves by the judgment of a future they see it as their task to bring about. Superstars seek success in a technique for eliciting support; heroes pursue success as the outgowth of their inner values." As the author states, "Winston Churchill was a hero." Highly recommended!
  Upper elem & up

- **Winston Churchill** - World Leaders Past & Present, by Judith Rodgers
  This is an excellent biography of one of the greatest statesmen of the twentieth century. The photographs are fascinating! Highly Recommended.
  Junior High & up

- **The Story of Winston Churchill** by Alida Sims Malkus
  Winston Churchill undoubtedly led one of the most adventurous lives in modern times. This fascinating biography is filled with his daring exploits and his monumental courage.
  Mid elem & up

- **The Story of Atomic Energy** - A World Landmark Book, by Laura Fermi
  Written by the widow of the physicist who built the first uranium pile (to see if it was possible to cause an atomic chain reaction), this fascinating book not only shows the development of atomic theory, it also sets this story into its moment of history. The race to build the first atomic bomb in WWII led to the many peaceful uses of atomic energy, also. Highly recommended! **Junior High & up**

- **Journey to America** by Sonia Levitin
  This historical fiction book, a winner of the National Jewish Book award, tells the story of a mother and three young daughters who flee Germany in 1938. The father has gone on ahead to make it possible for the family to come to America. Riveting! **Upper elem & up**

- **Air War Against Hitler's Germany** - American Heritage Junior Library, by Stephen W. Sears
  Filled with photos, maps, and illustrations, this excellent book describes the battle in the air between the Allies and Nazi Germany. Fascinating! **Upper elem & up**

- **Carrier War in the Pacific** - American Heritage Junior Library, by Stephen W. Sears
  Admiral Isoroku Yamamot, commander in chief of the Imperial Japanese Navy, in 1942 wrote, "In the last analysis, the success or failure of our entire strategy in the Pacific will be determined by whether or not we succeed in destroying the U.S. fleet, more particularly, its carrier task forces." This book tells the story of the war waged on sea and in the air. Highly recommended! **Upper elem & up**

- **Rescue in Denmark** by Harold Flender
  From the introduction - "In October 1943, the Nazis decided to round up Denmark's eight thouand Jews for shipment to the death camps. The entire country acted as an underground movement to ferry the eight thousand to Sweden. It was one of the few times that Eichmann had been frustrated. He visited Copenhagen in a rage - but to no avail. The Jews were saved." This is one of the most amazing stories from WWII! **Junior High & Up**

- **Dates with Destiny - The 100 Most Important Dates in Church History**
  by A. Kenneth Curtis, J. Stephen Lang, and Randy Petersen
  Beginning with the year 64 in Rome and continuing to 1976, this book is filled with short descriptions of events and people within the Church. For this chapter read about Dietrich Bonhoeffer. Highly recommended! **Upper elem & up**

- **From Jerusalem to Irian Jaya - A Biographical History of Christian Missions**
  by Ruth A. Tucker
  This is the best book on the history of world missions available. Included are short biographies of missionaries all over the world, categorized by their geographical area of service. I consider this an indispensable resource for the study of **World Empires, World Missions, World Wars**. For this chapter read pages 249 - 253. Highly recommended! **Upper elem & up**

- **Rees Howells - Intercessor** by Norman Grubb
  Deeply impacted by the 1904 Welsh Revival, Rees Howells then went to Africa and was used mightily by God in revival there. The end of the book refers to the dramatic answers to his intercessory prayers during World War II. Life-changing! **Junior High & up**

- **Lord of the Rings** by J.R.R. Tolkien
  Classic literature that portrays the reality of battling evil. **Junior High & up**

- **Audio: Bonhoeffer - The Cost of Freedom**
  This production from Focus on the Family is stirring. Follow the life of Dietrich Bonhoeffer, a German theologian, from childhood to his execution just before the end of WWII. His life, his integrity, and his willingness to stand for what was right will change your life. Highly recommended! **Junior High & up**

- **Video: The Longest Day**
  This movie feels like a documentary in its depiction of D-Day. The German soldiers speak German with English subtitles! It shows the tenseness, the slender thread by which the Allies hung on in certain places, and the remarkable string of mistakes made by the Germans. Excellent! **Upper elem & up**

- **Video: Midway**
  There are numerous movies made about WWII. You may find some excellent documentaries of WWII, and some other Hollywood movies that are reasonably accurate. This one is a good depiction of the battle of Midway - if you can overlook the Hollywood additions to the story! It really shows how the Japanese made the wrong decisions about whether to put torpedoes or bombs on their planes. Warning: Because this is about military operations, the producers chose to include a certain amount of swearing. **Junior High & up**

- **Video: The Inn of the Sixth Happiness**
  The story of Gladys Awylward, this movie is somewhat romanticized for Hollywood, but it is an excellent portrayal of the conditions Gladys faced. **For the whole family!**

Talk Together

The Big Guns: Roosevelt and Churchill

- Listen to What in the **World's Going On Here?, Volume Two**, Tape Four. What was the most interesting aspect to you of World War Two that was mentioned? Why? What other questions about this time period would you like to have answered?
  History Journal: Write those questions down and, as you study more material, write the answers to your questions. Also, write short bios of the people you study whom you find interesting. Illustrate the bios.

- Two days after Germany attacked Poland, England declared war on Germany. Then for the next several months, nothing happened. This period of time is called the "phony war." Why do you suppose neither side attacked? What kind of attitude do you think the people in Europe had about the war during this time? Do you think the rest of Europe was prepared for what Germany was about to launch? Why or why not?

- If you read **The Hiding Place**, you will learn what it was like to live in Holland just prior to the war, as well as what the "blitzkrieg" was to the people who lived through it. If you had been living in Holland, Belgium, or France during this time, would you have been frightened? Why or why not? How did Corrie ten Boom's family deal with their fear? Could this have an affect on you today? Describe how.

- Why do you think the Japanese wanted to "liberate" other Asian people? Who were they being liberated from? Do you think the Asians wanted to be liberated? Why or why not? Why was America seen as the main stumbling block to Japanese goals in the Pacific?

- Would you label the rescue of Allied soldiers from Dunkirk a miracle? Why or why not? How does this situation demonstrate the power of God in human history? Do you think the soldiers were aware of God's intervention during this time? Why or why not? If you had been one of the soldiers, what would you have prayed to happen? Have you personally seen God answer your prayers? Describe how.

- Remembering how Germany signed an armistice which ended WWI, why do you think France was willing to sign an armistice with Germany in 1940? Do you think the Vichy government was a legitimate government? Why or why not? What do you think the attitude of the common people of France was toward the Vichy government? What was the Free French government? Where was it located? Which government do you think represented the needs and desires of the people?

- What do you think Hitler wanted to accomplish by bombing Britain? Why was Britain important to Hitler's goals? How did Churchill frustrate Hitler and inspire the British?

- If you read **Rees Howells: Intercessor**, you will discover how much prayer was offered up to God on behalf of Great Britain. How did the author believe that God answered prayer concerning the bombing of civilian targets? Why do you think Hitler changed his policy of bombing airports and military installations? Does this situation in history encourage you to pray for your country? Why or why not?

- When Hitler ended the bombing of Britain, he turned his sights to Russia. How did Operation Barbarossa become one of his greatest mistakes? How was this military operation similar to Napoleon's fight with Russia?

- Why did Japan attack Pearl Harbor? How did this affect the American government and the American people? Do you think it was a good idea for the U.S. to become involved in WWII? Why or why not?

- The battle at Midway has also been called miraculous. What miraculous occurences do you observe? What did the Japanese hope to accomplish at Midway? What did the Americans hope to accomplish? What happened? What do you think would have been the result of Japan winning this battle? How might this have affected WWII?

- The battle of El Alamein began in October, 1942. Winston Churchill said, "Before Alamein we never had a victory. After Alamein we never had a defeat." Imagine you had been living in England during the first two years of the war without seeing any major victories for the Allies. Would the success of this battle have been important to you? Why or why not? Look at a map. How close to Palestine was El Alamein? If you had been a Jew living during this time, how important would this battle have been to you?

- Military historians have said that it is impossible to win a war only with airplanes - soldiers on the ground are required for victory. Imagine the logistical and tactical difficulties facing the Allies as they prepared for the invasion of Normandy (D-Day). What kinds of obstacles did they face? List some of the necessary supplies they needed to get ashore. Why weren't Allied soldiers already on the European Continent? How difficult do you think it was for Hitler's soldiers to defend the coastline? What mistakes did the German High Command make?

- The development of the atomic bomb ushered the world into the "Atomic Age" - for good and for evil. Why do you think President Harry Truman decided to drop atomic bombs on Hiroshima and Nagasaki? Do you think his decision was wise or foolish? What did his advisors tell him about the length of time and the number of lives needed in order to subdue Japan? If you had been the U.S. President, do you think you would have come to the same decision? Why or why not?

- Gladys Aylward was a small, poorly educated, English servant girl who felt that God had called her to China. After her admittance to the China Inland Mission school (which trained people in England for missionary work in China), she was informed that she was too old and too ignorant to learn Chinese. This only delayed her eventual trip to China. Do you think Gladys was courageous in continuing to follow the Lord's leading? Why or why not? Do you think God honored her courage and determination? Why or why not? How does her story challenge you today?

- WWII was the scene of unbelievable atrocities commited against many ethnic people groups, including the Jews. What was the "Holocaust"? Why do you think people allowed it to happen? What was the price for harboring Jews? If you had been living during this time, do you think you would have risked your life to help them? Why or why not? Are there situations in the world today that are similar to this situation? Are there ways you can help protect those who are being destroyed in "ethnic cleansings"? Describe how you and your family could make a difference.

- Consider the Treaty of Versailles at the end of WWI. Was there a difference in how the enemies of the Allies were treated at the end of WWII? Describe the difference. How did this affect Japan, Germany and Italy? Do you think this difference was appropriate and good? Why or why not?

Teaching Time!

Seminar Outline

I. Beginning of World War II
    A. German tanks roll into Poland - September 1, 1939
    B. England Declares War - September 3, 1939
        1. Winston Churchill, Lord of the Admiralty
        2. "Winston is back"
    C. The Phony War - September - May 1940
        1. Nobody does anything
        2. Winter season
        3. France has the Maginot Line
    D. The Blitzkrieg Attack - May 1940
        1. Germans invade the Netherlands, Belgium and France
        2. Neville Chamberlain steps down from office
            a. Churchill made Prime Minister in 1940
        3. Leads to the miracle of Dunkirk

II. Preparation for war in Asia
    A. Japan's top war minister, Tojo
    B. Samurai Code of Honor
        1. Save face
        2. Better to die than to lose
    C. Non-Asians had no right to interfere in Asia
        1. "Liberate" Asians
        2. Set up Japanese colonies
        3. Taken by conquest
    D. America seen as main stumbling block to Japanese
        1. Humiliation by Commodore Perry
        2. "Japan's Mortal Enemy"

III. Events in WWII
    A. Evacuation from Dunkirk - May 26-June 4, 1940
        1. 43-mile corridor with 400,000 Allied soldiers trapped
        2. Dunkirk only remaining free port
        3. Miracle was the only hope
        4. Churchill thought perhaps 30,000 might be saved
        5. Rees Howells, Intercessor, prays for the miracle
        6. English Channel calm for 9 days - miraculous!
        7. Hitler halts the panzers unexpectedly - May 24
        8. Three days to form a guarded perimeter - closing the corridor
        9. 338,000 Allied troops saved in 9 days
            a. English navy, plus every floating boat, barge, yacht
            b. Heavy fog prevents Luftwaffe from finding targets
    B. France signs Armistice with Germany - June 22, 1940

       1. Vichy government
       2. Free French in Britan

C. Battle of Britain begins - August 1940
       1. Hitler's policy - bomb Britain
       2. Churchill's policy - "Never give in! Never give in! Never give in!"
       3. Nazis concentrate on airports, military installations at first
       4. Change to bombing civilian targets
       5. Final day of bombing - answer to prayer!
       6. Divine Intervention

D. Operation Barbarossa - June 22, 1941
       1. German invasion of Soviet Union
       2. Same day of the year as Napoleon's invasion
       3. Cost Hitler greatly

E. Japanese attack on Pearl Harbor - December 7, 1941
       1. U.S. enters war
       2. Raid on Tokyo - April 18, 1942

F. Battle of Midway - June 4, 1942
       1. Strategic to the United States
       2. U.S. figures out the Japanese cipher code
          a. Learns that the place of battle would be Midway
          b. Learns the date of the battle
       3. Turning point of the War in the Pacific

G. Battle of El Alamein begins - Africa - October 1942
       1. Rommel, the German general, very successful
       2. Allies retreat to just outside Cairo - longest retreat in British history
       3. Prayer
       4. Montgomery appointed the head of the British soldiers
       5. First major Allied victory in WWII - Turning point of the war

"Before Alamein we never had a victory. After Alamein we never had a defeat."
Winston Churchill

H. German 6th Army surrenders at Battle of Stalingrad - January 1943
I. D-Day - June 1944
       1. Miracle to get back onto the Continent
       2. Millions of soldiers and tons of equipment brought back
J. U.S. returns to the Phillipines, reclaiming Asian islands
K. Hitler commits suicide - April 30, 1945
L. VE Day Europe - May 8
M. Atomic bomb developed
       1. To avoid another year of war with Japan
       2. Dropped on Hiroshima - August 6
       3. Dropped on Nagasaki - August 9
N. Japan surrenders, WWII ends - August 14, 1945

Timeline

On your timeline, mark the Phony War, the Blitzkrieg, the Battle of Britain, the War in the Pacific, the War in North Africa, the Battle of El Alamein, the Battle of Stalingrad, D-Day, VE Day, the atomic bombs at Hiroshima and Nagasaki, and the end of WWII.

Research & Reporting

- Find one of the books listed at the beginning of this unit, along with the encyclopedia or other history resource book, for basic information on World War II. Write a report detailing what you learn.

- Research and report on the Maginot Line in France. Include details on its construction, defenses, and troops. Show how the Germans were able to render the Maginot barrier ineffective.

- Study the military tactics of the German blitzkrieg. Make a chart or diagram showing how the blitzkrieg worked and why no one was able to withstand it.

- Research and report on the bombing of Britain during the Battle of Britain. Show the strategy of the Germans, how this changed over time, and the defenses of the British. Include Winston Churchill's policy towards Hitler.

- Research and report on the sinking of the Bismarck by the British. Include the overall plan of the Germans to isolate England by rendering her ineffective in the Atlantic.

- The rescue of 338,000 Allied soldiers from the shores of Dunkirk is one of the most amazing military operations in history. Research and report on what transpired in Belgium and France to require this rescue, who was involved, and how the Germans responded.

- Research and report on Operation Barbarossa - the Nazi invasion of Russia. What were the results for the German army? - For the Russians?

- Research and report on the bombing of Pearl Harbor by Japan. Include details on why this surprise attack was deemed necessary by the Japanese, what the strategies were for accomplishing it, the results for the U.S. Navy, and the effect it had upon U.S. involvement in WWII.

- Study and make a chart or diagram showing U.S. retaliation in the bombing of Tokyo. Include the staging area (what ships were involved), the target areas, and the success of the mission.

- After the bombing of Pearl Harbor, the U.S. government set up internment camps for Japanese-American citizens. Research and report on these camps. What was their purpose? Was there evidence that supported the building of these camps? What was the effect upon the Japanese-Americans who were confined?

- Research and report on the Battle of Midway. You might wish to include a diagram showing the Japanese fleet, Midway Island, and the U.S. ships. Explain the significance of the decision to rearm the Japanese planes with torpedoes. Show why this was the turning point of the war in the Pacific.

- Research and report on the Battle of El Alamein. What would have been the significance of a German victory in this area? (Hint: Consider its geographical location.)

- D-Day was the beginning of the end for the Third Reich. Research and report on what was involved in planning and executing this military invasion. Include the strategies used to fool the Germans as to place and time for the invasion. Answer the question, "Why was D-Day necessary?"

- Research and report on the concentration camps used by the Nazis. You may wish to include information from **The Hiding Place** by Corrie ten Boom. What was the purpose of these camps? What was the Final Solution? Who was considered to be valueless in Nazi Germany?

- Research and report on the underground "Resistance" during WWII. What did people in the Resistance do? How did they affect the war effort? What were some of the political leanings of people in the Resistance? How did the Nazis fight the Resistance?

- On April 30, 1945, Adolf Hitler committed suicide. Study and write about the ending of the war in Europe. How did Germany come to be divided up among the Russians, French, British, and U.S.? What was the purpose of occupation? What was the actual effect? What happened in Italy?

- Research and report on the Nuremburg Trials. What was the purpose? Who were the accused? For what crimes were they accused? What excuses for their crimes did they offer? Who were the plaintiffs? What were the results of these trials?

- Research and report on the war in the Philippines and General Douglas MacArthur. Who was MacArthur addressing when he said, "I shall return"? How did he fulfill this promise, and how long did it take?

- Research and report on the Flying Tigers and the war in China. Include information on Japan's strategies for defeating China, and how China responded. Who were the Flying Tigers and what part did they play in the defense of China? How were China's internal struggles between Nationalist and Communist forces affected by the war with Japan?

- Gladys Aylward, a little British parlourmaid, was the first European to became a Chinese citizen. Study her life and write a report showing the obstacles she faced in getting to the mission field as well as the work she did after arriving in China.

- Research and report on the Manhattan Project. Show the purposes atomic energy has for the military, and how it was used to end WWII. Contrast this with the peacetime uses of atomic energy.

Brain Stretchers

- Compare and contrast the German general, Rommel, with the British general, Montgomery, in the war in North Africa. How were they similar? How were they different? How were the retreating British soldiers affected by Montgomery's appointment to North Africa? Why was Rommel called, "The Desert Fox"?

- Winston Churchill said, "Before Alamein, we never had a victory. After Alamein, we never had a defeat." Analyze whether this was true, and if so, what were the reasons.

- There has been a resurgence of Nazism recently. Study and analyze the reasons for this return to a violent, defeated political philosophy. Devise a Christian response to those involved.

- One of the more fascinating stories of WWII concerns the "heavy water" factory in Norway which Hitler wanted to exploit for the purposes of building an atomic bomb. Research and report on the work of the Allied soldiers from Norway who were assigned the job of stopping him.

Vocabulary

blitzkrieg	miracle	siege	invasion
concentration camps	occupation	resistance	refugee
frogmen	paratroops	perimeter	statesman
atomic	carriers	underground	holocaust
invasion	evacuation	panzers	intercessor

In this unit there is a great emphasis on the terminology of WWII.

- Your assignment is to collect as many new military terms as you find in this unit's study, and define them.

Hands On!

**Maps
and
Mapping**

- Using an atlas, encyclopedia, or other resource locate the major locations of WWII. This would include the following: Dunkirk (in Belgium), the English Channel, Vichy (in France), Germany, Italy, Stalingrad (in Russia), British Somaliland, Egypt, Libya, El Alamein, Ethiopia, Tunisia, Algeria, Morocco, Pearl Harbor, Tokyo, Hiroshima, Nagasaki, Normandy (in France), Warsaw (in Poland), Guam, Malaya, Burma, Singapore, the Philippines, Midway Island, New Guinea, Solomon Islands, Guadalcanal, Mariana Islands, Marshall Islands, Iwo Jima, Okinawa.

- On a clean worksheet map, with colored markers, show the war in Europe, the battle of Britain, the battle of the Atlantic, the war in North Africa, the war in the Pacific, and the Normandy Invasion.

- Consult a relief map to discover the terrain found in the war of the Pacific and the war in North Africa (since we have studied the terrain of Europe already). Are there deserts, forest, mountains, islands? Label them. What kind of climate is typical in each of the different terrains? How did these different terrains and climates affect each side in the war?

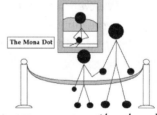

Art Appreciation

*During World War II, there was very little "serious" art created. However, every nation involved in WWII used poster art to capture the attention and secure the loyalty of its citizens. Poster art originally became a very popular form of art in Europe during the late 1800's with Henri de Toulouse-Lautrec. However, posters were (and are) an excellent form of advertising, and were powerfully used for spreading propaganda. See the example in **World Empires, World Missions, World Wars** unit seven, page 109.*

- Look up "World War II," "Poster," and "Propaganda" in the encyclopedia. What were some of the purposes for posters during WWII? Do you think they were effective? How are posters used today? Do you think they are effective? Do you consider this a true form of art? Why or why not?

- Look up "Toulouse-Lautrec" in the encyclopedia. How would you describe his art? Was his work similar to the Impressionists? Why or why not? Do you like his posters? Why or why not?

- Online, go to **http://www.internationalposter.com** and look at old posters.

Arts in Action

- Create a poster! Decide first on the purpose of the poster. It could be used to advertise an event, market a product (like, lemonade), support a politician, etc. Then decide what simple figures or emblems will best convey what you want to communicate. Consider the background, the wording, the colors. Remember that it needs to be clear in its message. Have fun!

- For your older students, if you want to be high-tech, go online to:
  http://www.arttoday.com or **http://www.eyewire.com** and download poster image graphics. Then create your poster and print it!

Architecture

"… OOPS!! …"

For this unit, like unit six, there is no architecture activity - everyone was too busy blowing things up to design new buildings.

Science

One of the potentially most damaging military technologies developed during WWII was that of rocketry. Germany was trying to gain the ability to launch long-range ballistic missiles against her enemies, while the Allies were also working on this technology. Unfortunately, for the Allies, the Germans had a scientist named Wernher von Braun working for them. Von Braun's interest was in space exploration, but the same rockets that would allow man to travel in space would also benefit the military who used them for weaponry. It was a blessing to the Allies that Germany did not develop the V-2 (guided missile) until the closing days of WWII - otherwise the outcome of the war might have been very different.

- Read more about Robert Goddard and Wernher von Braun, two of the most significant rocket scientists in history.

- Learn the Newtonian principle behind rockets!
  Isaac Newton said that for every action there is an opposite and equal reaction.
  How does this work in rocketry? Try this: Blow up a balloon and let it go. Why does it fly forward?
  When you blow up a balloon and hold the end shut, all the air stays inside the balloon - nothing is moving. But, when you let go of the end, the action of the air rushing out in one direction causes an equal reaction in the other direction. To see it more clearly, thread a long piece of fishing line through a straw. Tie each end of the fishing line to chairs across the room from each other. Blow up the balloon again, and have someone else tape the balloon to the straw in a couple of places. Now let go of your balloon - in other words, launch your "rocket."

- **Make it Work! Flight** by Jack Challoner shows how to make a model space shuttle rocket. Go for it!

Music

Bela Bartok was one of the most significant and influential composers of the twentieth century. His most important works were composed from 1930 to 1945. Bartok was from Eastern Europe (born in Hungary, though now it is considered to be Rumania), and was vocal in his denunciation of Nazi Germany. He fled Hungary in 1939 because of the "robbery and murder of Nazism," ending up eventually in New York.

The music of Bartok derives much of its melodic line and rhythmic irregularities from the folk songs and gypsy music of Eastern Europe which he spent years collecting. There is a tremendous sense of driving rhythmic energy in this music. Harmonically, it is challenging to the ear because Bartok used chords and harmonies that were either derived from Eastern European sources or made up to follow his own system. You may have heard musicians talking about how a piece of music was written in a particular "key" (like, the "Key of A"). Bartok expanded that concept, incorporating such a variety of harmonic techniques that the notion of the "key" is all but lost. You will notice that his music sounds different than the other composers we have named!

- Listen to Bartok's **Concerto for Orchestra** (1943), composed while he was dying of leukemia. This is perhaps the most popular of his works today. Do you hear the sounds of war in this music? (Remember that WWII was still raging.) How would you describe this music? How is it different from the other composers you have studied?

- For further study in this time period, follow the phenomenon of musical theatre that swept the world, beginning in the 1940's. Listen to, or watch, a recording of **Oklahoma** or **The Sound of Music**.

Cooking

Douglas MacArthur, during the war in the Pacific, told the people of the Philippines, "I shall return"... And you will return to these treats once you try them!

Camote Frito - Deep-Fried Sweet Potato Chips

2 pounds sweet potatoes   Oil for deep-frying
  (it's easier if they are long and cylindrical)   Powdered sugar

CAUTION: *Adult supervision required!*

Peel the sweet potatoes and cut them crosswise into paper-thin slices. Drop the slices into a bowl filled with cold water and let them soak for about 15 minutes.

Pour oil into a deep fryer or large, heavy saucepan to a depth of 2 to 3 inches and heat it until it reaches a temperature of 375 degrees on a deep-frying thermometer.

Just before frying, drain the slices and pat them completely dry. Fry the potatoes in 3 batches - slowly immersing them into the hot oil. Fry for 3 to 4 minutes, or until they turn a golden color. As they brown, transfer the slices to paper towels to drain. Serve warm, sprinkled lightly with powdered sugar. YUM!

Idea Time

Creative Writing

- As a reporter for "France Today," you have been assigned to interview the French soldiers at the Maginot Line, as well as local French citizens, during what has become known as the "Phony War." Are the people concerned about Germany's intentions? Help your readers by getting the scoop on this puzzling issue!

- Finish this poem about the miracle rescue of Dunkirk:

  Our circumstance was hopeless
  We despaired on the sandy beach...

- The Allies have asked you to write your ideas on how to fool the Germans about Operation Overlord (the plans for the D-Day invasion). Knowing that the Germans are expecting some sort of invasion, it is up to you to point them in the wrong direction. Good luck!

- The television news program, "Miracles Today," has asked you to interview Corrie ten Boom about her experiences in the German concentration camp. Be sure to ask her about the bottle of vitamins!

- As a German soldier with Rommel in North Africa, write a letter home to your family describing your experiences chasing Allies. You might want to include what you have heard through the grapevine about the new British commander, Montgomery.

Art

- Draw a political cartoon showing how the powerful Japanese navy was beaten by a handful of U.S. ships during the miraculous battle of Midway.

Drama

- Re-enact the story of Gladys Aylward's life - failure at the missionary school, adventure across Russia, work for the Mandarin, and the rescue of the orphaned children during the war. It will be more fun if you add costumes!

The Big Picture

- WWII is a study in the truth of Corrie ten Boom's words: "There is no darkness so great that God's love is not greater still." Plan a series of contrasts through drama, speeches, art, etc. which will show this truth for your family, friends, and neighbors. Then share with one another over a meal how to apply this to your own lives and present day circumstances.

Unit Nine

The Cold War, the Korean War, Israel & Unto the Uttermost Parts...

Korea

Unit Objectives:

- To discover the establishment of the nation of Israel in 1948, and the Arab response;

- to learn about the decolonization of Africa after WWII;

- to understand the Cold War, the Korean War, and the function of the United Nations;

- to read about the struggle between the Nationalists and Communists in China, and the result;

- to study missionaries after WWII - behind the Iron Curtain, in the Pacific with cargo cults, in the jungles, and in the cities.

Meet the People & Study the Countries:

Here are some people you might meet in this unit:

In the Church:

Brother Andrew	Nate Saint	Francis & Edith Schaeffer
Jim Elliot	Don Richardson	John Rush

In the World:

Chaim Weizmann	David Ben-Gurion	Anwar Sadat
Haile Selassie	Nkrumah	Konrad Adenauer
Chiang Kai-Shek	Mao Zedong	

You might wish to study one of these places in depth during this unit:

African Nations	Israel	Egypt
Korea	China/Taiwan	Papua New Guinea

- **The Holy Bible**
  Psalm 126; Isaiah 35:10, 43:5-7; Jeremiah 46:27-28; Matthew 5:43-48; John 12:24-26, 15:13

- **Chaim Weizmann** - World Leaders Past & Present, by Richard Amdur
  This is the biography of a Russian Jew who studied science in Germany, moved to England, and, by his scientific assistance to the British during WWI, gained the Balfour Declaration of 1917. The Balfour Declaration guaranteed the Jews a national homeland in Palestine. Chaim Weizmann, a fascinating personality, was the first elected president of the new nation of Israel. Highly recommended! **Junior High & up**

- **Ben-Gurion and the Birth of Israel** - A World Landmark Book, by Joan Comay
  David Ben-Gurion, born in Poland in 1886, moved to Palestine in 1906 along with many other Jewish settlers. His life revolved around the building up and establishing of Israel as a nation. He was, in fact, the one to pronounce the birth of Israel to the world in 1948 as the Arab nations were beginning to attack Tel-Aviv. Highly recommended! **Upper elem & up**

- **David Ben-Gurion** - World Leaders Past & Present, by John J. Vail
  Another in this excellent series of biographies for older students, this title focuses on the man known as the founding father of his country. Highly recommended! **Junior High & up**

- **Israel - New People in an Old Land** by Lily Edelman
  Revised in 1969, this is an excellent look at Israel for children. It includes a description of the different people groups who make up Israel, an overview of the geography, working in Israel, and the Hebrew Alphabet. **Upper elem & up**

- **Israel** - Cultures of the World Series, by Jill duBois
  This series of books gives a brief overview of the country's history, its geography, and culture. An excellent "primer" for discovering more about modern day Israel and the people who live there - Arabs and Jews. **Mid elem & up**

- **Anwar Sadat** - World Leaders Past & Present, by Patricia Aufderheide
This is the biography of Egypt's great soldier and statesman, Anwar Sadat. It is fascinating to discover how he went from pursuing war with the Jews to pursuing peace.
Junior High & up

- **The Arab/Israeli Conflict** by Paul J. Deegan
The situation in the Middle East is complex and many-faceted. This book describes many of the involved issues in terms children can understand. **Mid elem & up**

- **The Berlin Wall - How it Rose and Why it Fell** by Doris M. Epler
This excellent book traces the history of the Cold War in Germany, beginning with WWII. It includes the Berlin airlift, and the famous speech made by President John F. Kennedy in Berlin just months before his assassination. Highly recommended! **Upper elem & up**

- **Konrad Adenauer** - World Leaders Past & Present, by Edythe Cudlipp
Elected Chancellor of the Federal Republic of Germany in 1949, Adenauer's life of service to Germany spans from before the first world war until 1963. This biography helps to show what transpired in this country after the end of WWII. **Junior High & up**

- **Brother Andrew** - Men of Faith Series, by Dan Wooding
Subtitled, "The remarkable story of the man who has come to be known as God's Smuggler," this is the biography of a man used by God to penetrate the communist countries of the world with Bibles for the persecuted Church. Fascinating! **Upper elem & up**

- **God's Smuggler** by Brother Andrew
This is one of the most profound books our family has ever read. I highly recommend this autobiography of Brother Andrew! **Upper elem & up**

- **The War in Korea** - A World Landmark Book, by Robert Leckie
The Korean War, 1950-1953, is explained in an understandable way in this excellent account. The emerging role of the United Nations becomes evident in the story of this war. Highly recommended! **Upper elem & up**

- **Korea** - Enchantment of the World Series, by Sylvia McNair
This series of books gives a brief overview of the country's history, its geography, and culture. An excellent "primer" for discovering more about Korea and the Korean people.
Mid elem & up

- **The United Nations in War and Peace** - A World Landmark Book, by T.R. Fehrenbach
If you can locate this book, it is an excellent "primer" of world events after the end of WWII (up to 1965) written from the perspective of the development of the United Nations. Learn about the Cold War, the Partition in Palestine, the Korean War, the Suez Canal Crisis, the Hungarian revolt, the Cuban missile crisis, and the start of the Vietnam War. Highly recommended! **Upper elem & up**

- **Chiang Kai-Shek** - World Leaders Past & Present, by Sean Dolan
  Chiang Kai-Shek worked under Sun Yat-Sen, and after Sun Yat-Sen's death, became the head of the Guomindang (Nationalist Party) in 1925. After WWII, through the corruption of his government and his strong-arm tactics toward dissenters, he lost China to the Communists under Mao Zedong. An excellent biography.   **Junior High & up**

- **Mao Zedong** - World Leaders Past & Present, by Hedda Garza
  This is the man who made China an influential world power. He was a Communist revolutionary. He said, "A revolution is not a dinner party, or writing an essay, or painting a picture, or doing embroidery; it cannot be so refined, so leisurely and gentle, so temperate, kind, courteous, restrained and magnanimous. A revolution is an insurrection, an act of violence by which one class overthrows another." This attitude explains much of what has taken place in China since 1949.   **Junior High & up**

- **China's Long March - 6,000 Miles of Danger** by Jean Fritz
  Jean Fritz is a noted children's author, and this book is a wonderful example of her ability to tell a story. She traveled to China in 1986 to talk to survivors of the Long March (when the Communist Chinese fled to the mountains). This book is their story.   **Upper elem & up**

- **The Long March - Red China Under Chairman Mao** by Don Lawson
  This is a fantastic book! Beginning with the trial of the Gang of Four (including Mao's widow), it describes Mao's childhood, the Long March, the Communist Revolution, Mao's mistakes, and the impact he had upon China. Highly recommended!   **Upper elem & up**

- **Haile Selassie** - World Leaders Past & Present, by Askale Negash
  Emperor of Ethiopia from 1920 until 1974 (in exile from 1936 - 1941), this was one of the most remarkable leaders in the 20th century. Considered the elder African statesman during the decolonization of much of Africa, his influence was critically important. Excellent!
  Junior High & up

- **Kwame Nkrumah** - World Leaders Past & Present, by Douglas Kellner
  The founder of modern Ghana and one of the architects of the pan-African movement (to end colonial rule), Nkrumah was a significant player in African politics. Decolonization in Africa is a multi-faceted study, involving economics, politics, tribal loyalties, and military rule. This book and the one listed above will give the student a good foundation for learning about decolonization.   **Junior High & up**

- **Assassins in the Cathedral** - Trailblazer Books, by Dave & Neta Jackson
  This is a historical fiction account of Festo Kivengere, bishop in Uganda during Idi Amin's rule. It will help your student not only understand some of the difficulties faced by the African countries, with warring tribes coexisting side by side, but it will show the profound importance of forgiveness. Excellent!   **Mid elem & up**

- **Nate Saint** - Christian Heroes Then and Now, by Janet & Geoff Benge
  Wonderfully written, this series of Christian biographies is fascinating, factual, and historically accurate. Nate Saint was the missionary aviator who flew the group of missionaries (including Jim Elliot) to reach the Auca Indians. His powerful testimony is movingly portrayed in this excellent book. Highly recommended! **Mid elem & up**

- **Jungle Pilot** by Russell T. Hitt
  This is the updated edition of the missionary classic about the martyrdom of Nate Saint. Included are photos, plus a new epilogue written by Nate's son, Stephen, who returned to the jungles of Ecuador to report the remarkable progress in the work with the Aucas. Highly recommended! **Upper elem & up**

- **Jim Elliot** - Christian Heroes Then and Now, by Janet & Geoff Benge
  Wonderfully written, this series of Christian biographies is fascinating, factual, and historically accurate. Jim Elliot was an American missionary in Ecuador, who gave his life so that the Auca Indians might know Jesus. Highly recommended! **Mid elem & up**

- **Through Gates of Splendor** by Elisabeth Elliot
  Jim Elliot's story has motivated many people to live a sacrificial life for the sake of Jesus. He was an American missionary who wanted to live his life fully for Jesus, regardless of the cost. He was martyred in 1956 while attempting to reach a stone-age tribe in Ecuador - the Auca Indians. This powerful book was written by his widow. Highly recommended! **Junior High & up**

- **Dayuma - Life under Waorani Spears** by Ethel Emily Wallis
  If you are going to read about Jim Elliot or Nate Saint, you MUST read this book! It tells what happened among the Aucas after the martyrdom of the missionaries in 1956. All praise and glory to our God, who truly works all things together for good for those that love God and are the called according to His purposes! Highly recommended! **Upper elem & up**

- **Francis & Edith Schaeffer** - Women & Men of Faith Series, by L.G. Parkhurst, Jr.
  Subtitled, "Christian missionary apologists who challenged a world of skeptics to faith," this is the biography of two of the most influential Christians of the twentieth century. Highly recommended! **Upper elem & up**

- **L'Abri** by Edith Schaeffer
  The autobiographical story of how God took an American couple to Europe immediately after WWII to begin a ministry to skeptics and intellectuals. Life-changing! **Upper elem & up**

- **Tapestry** by Francis and Edith Schaeffer
  One of the most treasured books on my shelf, this is the story of Francis and Edith Schaeffer. Told in rich detail, her book describes how God worked mightily in their lives to provide a refuge, a "l'abri," for a world disillusioned by World War II and liberal theology. It is out-of-print, but worth the search. Highly recommended! **Junior High & up**

- **The Man with the Bird on His Head** - International Adventures, by John Rush & Abbe Anderson
Available through YWAM Publishing, this is one of the most amazing missionary stories of the twentieth century! If you are going to read about John Paton, you MUST read this story, too. It concerns a tribal group on Tanna in the South Pacific who became a "cargo cult" after WWII. They were known as the John Frum people, because they were waiting for John Frum to tell them of spiritual truths. (You might enjoy knowing that John Rush is a homeschooling dad.) Absolutely amazing!! Highly recommended!! **Upper elem & up**

- **Peace Child** by Don Richardson
One of the most amazing books you will ever read, this is the true autobiographical story of a missionary couple who ministered to a head-hunting tribe in Irian Jaya. This cannibalistic tribe esteemed treachery and murder. When the story of Jesus was explained, Judas Iscariot, not Jesus, was the hero to them! Providentially, God placed an incredible "redemptive analogy" within their culture which brought them to a deep, life-changing understanding of the Gospel. (Parents: The opening scenes are fairly gruesome. Please read them first.) Highly recommended! **Junior High & up**

- **The Chronicles of Narnia** by C.S. Lewis
Classic literature for children and adults alike, these are allegorical stories of the Kingdom of God. Wonderful! **Great Read Aloud**

- **Dates with Destiny - The 100 Most Important Dates in Church History** by A. Kenneth Curtis, J. Stephen Lang, and Randy Petersen
Beginning with the year 64 in Rome and continuing to 1976, this book is filled with short descriptions of events and people within the Church. For this chapter read about the Chinese Church during the Cultural Revolution. Highly recommended! **Upper elem & up**

- **From Jerusalem to Irian Jaya - A Biographical History of Christian Missions** by Ruth A. Tucker
This is the best book on the history of world missions available. Included are short biographies of missionaries all over the world, categorized by their geographical area of service. I consider this an indispensable resource for the study of **World Empires, World Missions, World Wars**. For this chapter read pages 398 - 400, 472 - 474, 481 - 485. Highly recommended! **Upper elem & up**

- **The Military History of the Korean War** by S. L. A. Marshall
Written for children by a brigadier general, operations analyst in Korea, this is a well-written, fascinating description of the Korean War. **Upper elem & up**

- **The Korean War** - Turning Points in American History, by Carter Smith
This is another excellent book for children describing the various aspects of the Korean War. **Upper elem & up**

Talk Together

Checkpoint Charlie

- Listen to **What in the World's Going On Here?, Volume Two**, Tape Four, Side Two. What was the most interesting aspect to you of the establishment of Israel as a nation that was mentioned? Why? What other questions about this time period would you like to have answered?
  History Journal: Write those questions down and, as you study more material, write the answers to your questions. Also, write short bios of the people you study whom you find interesting. Illustrate the bios.

- Listen to **True Tales from the Times of World Empires, World Missions, World Wars**, Side Two. What were the most interesting aspects to you of the Korean War or the Cold War that were mentioned? Why? What questions do you have about this time period that you would like to learn more about?

- Why do you think the Jews of Europe were singled out by Hitler for extermination? What were some of the attitudes and actions of other Europeans to this policy? What was the response by the world to the Jews after the extent of the Holocaust was known at the close of World War II? Do you think the guilt people felt might have influenced the vote at the U.N. for "partition" in Palestine? Why or why not?

- Describe Britain's involvement in Palestine. Do you think they were for or against the establishment of a new nation of Israel? Why?

- Imagine you had been a Jew living in Palestine on May 14, 1948. How would you feel about the declaration of Israel as a nation? Defend your position on the rightness or wrongness of this declaration. What would be your expectation of the reaction of the surrounding Arab countries?

- Imagine you had been an Arab living in Palestine on May 14, 1948. How would you feel about the declaration of Israel as a nation? Defend your position on the rightness or wrongness of this declaration. What would be your expectation of the reaction of the surrounding Arab countries?

- What might be some of the reasons that the surrounding Arab countries would fight to "push Israel into the sea"? (Hint: Consider Ishmael & Isaac.)

- Why do you think the African colonies were among the last European colonies to be given their independence? How did the African colonies differ from India? - From Australia and New Zealand? - From Southeast Asian colonies? - From Indonesia?

- Do you think colonization was beneficial to the people of Africa? Why or why not? Do you think decolonization was beneficial to the people of Africa? Why or why not? Do you think the decolonization of Africa was beneficial to the European nations who had formerly colonized them? Why or why not?

- South Africa and Algeria were in a different situation than the other African nations. Britain and France had poured money, settlers, and armies into these respective colonies, and were loathe to give them up. Why do you suppose these two African countries were more closely aligned with Europe? (Hint: Consider geography and history.)

- The United Nations was formed after World War II to provide a forum for resolving conflicts between nations without the necessity of war. Read about the beginning years of the United Nations and then discuss whether the U.N. has fulfilled its original goals. Does the U.N. function today as it was originally intended? Why or why not? What do you think of the U.N.? Why?

- "Cold War" is the term used to describe the high level of tension between the Communist bloc countries and the West after World War II. What are some of the reasons that East and West did not engage in another full scale world war but fought "limited" wars, such as Korea and Viet Nam instead? In what ways has that situation changed today?

- Why and when was the Berlin Wall built? Why and when did it come down? How would the Berlin Wall be a picture of relations between the East and West during the Cold War?

- Read about Brother Andrew. Why do you think the Communist countries did not allow Bibles to be brought into their lands? Why was it critically necessary for the churches under Communist regimes to have Bibles? Do you think it was right for Brother Andrew to smuggle Bibles into Communist countries? Why or why not? How does this impact the way you value your own Bible?

- General Douglas MacArthur was fired during the Korean War by President Truman because of his criticisms of Truman's policy of a limited war. Read more about this situation and then discuss whether you think MacArthur was right in his opinion. What might have happened if the U.N. had shown more force in Korea? Do you think President Truman showed wisdom or cowardice? Defend your opinion.

- Why do you think the Korean War happened? What were the contributing causes? (Hint: What country was governing Korea just prior to WWII? What happened after WWII? Why do you think China was involved? How did the Communist Revolution in China affect this situation?)

- Why do you think China became a Communist country? Read more about Chiang Kai-Shek and Mao Zedong to answer this question. How did life for the people of China change after the Revolution?

- How were the China Inland Mission and other missionary organizations in China affected by the Communist Revolution? What happened to the churches and Christians in China? Has this changed? Find resources to read more about the house church movement in China today. (The ministry, Voice of the Martyrs, is an excellent place to start your search.) What do you think happens to the Church during times of persecution? Has this happened in China?

- Jim Elliot and four other missionaries went to a beach on the Curaray river in the jungles of Ecuador to try to make contact with a Stone-Age tribe called the Waorani (known to their enemies as the Aucas). This tribe had killed everyone who had ever come into their territory, so the danger to the missionaries was extreme. After a brief contact with three of the tribespeople, the missionaries had high expectations. However, their group also was killed by the Waorani. When officials searched the area (to find the bodies), they found guns belonging to the missionaries. Since the guns had not been used, we know that they could have defended themselves but chose instead to give up their lives. Why do you think they did this? What would the impact to the Waoranis have been if the missionaries had defended themselves with guns? Read John 15:13 and discuss how this Scripture applies to the situation. What happened to the Waorani after the martyrdom of the five missionaries? (Hint: **Read Dayuma - Life Under Waorani Spears**, by Ethel Emily Wallis to answer this question.)

- Don Richardson, in his book, **Peace Child**, tells the amazing story of a cannibalistic, treacherous tribe in Iryan Jaya which had within its cultural lore a "redemptive analogy." This analogy allowed the tribe to move from honoring Judas Iscariot in his role as betrayer of Christ to abhorring his act when they understood that Jesus was the "peace child" of God. Read the book and discuss the concept of "redemptive analogy." How did this concept get into a tribal people's oral history? What are the implications of this for missionaries? Are there implications for your own culture and society? For further study on this fascinating concept, read **Eternity in Their Hearts**, by Don Richardson.

- Why do you think L'Abri (the home and ministry of Francis & Edith Schaeffer) played such a vital role in Christianity after WWII?

Teaching Time!

Seminar Outline

I. End of World War II
    A. Uncovered Holocaust horrors
        1. 6 million Jews exterminated
        2. Hitler's Final Solution
    B. Palestine
        1. UN solution - Partition
            a. Arabs get some land
            b. Jews get some land
        2. Britain withdrew May 14, 1948
            a. Many terrorist acts committed by both sides
            b. "If you will it, it is not dream." Theodor Herzl
        3. David Ben-Gurion proclaimed new state of Israel on May 14, 1948
            a. 2,000 years without a homeland
            b. God providentially made a way
        4. Arabs disagreed
            a. Tried to push Israel into the sea
            b. Not successful
        5. Cease-fire - 1949

Timeline

On your timeline, mark the establishment of Israel as a nation in 1948, the period of the Cold War, the Korean War, the establishment of the U.N., the Communist Revolution in China, the decolonization of the various African countries, Jim Elliot, Brother Andrew, and Francis and Edith Schaeffer.

Research & Reporting

- Find one of the books listed at the beginning of this unit, along with the encyclopedia or other history resource book, for basic information on the establishment of Israel as a nation in 1948. Write a report detailing the U.N. vote, the response of the Arab nations, and the ways in which the Jews not only defended themselves but built their nation.

- Research and report on the Holocaust of WWII. Include information about Denmark's response to the Nazi command to turn over their Jews, and people (like Corrie ten Boom) who defied the Nazis by hiding Jews in their homes. Show the aftermath of the Holocaust for the survivors, and how they were able to trace other family members.

- Research and report on the manhunt for Nazi criminals carried on for decades by dedicated Jews. Show their successes, the areas of the world where Nazis have tried to hide, and how the Israelis have worked to bring them to justice.

- Study and write about the establishment of Israel as a nation in 1948. Include information on the U.N. vote, the attack by Arab nations, and the form of government in Israel.

- Research and report on the history of Israel since 1948 until today. How many wars have been fought, and what were the results of these wars? Indicate the different places in the world Jews have left to come to Israel. What are the concerns and conflicts in Israel today?

- Research and report on the history of any one of the Arab nations from the end of WWI until today. What form of government do they have? What are the major sources of income? What is life like for the citizens of this country? What are the concerns and conflicts in this county today?

- Study and write about the Berlin Airlift and the Berlin Wall - both caused by the Cold War. What were the situations which brought each into existence, and what caused them to end?

- Research and report on the Iron Curtain. What does this term refer to? What countries were behind the Iron Curtain? How were they affected by this? What caused the Iron Curtain to come down? How has this affected the countries involved? What is the relationship of the Berlin Wall to the Iron Curtain?

- Research and report on Germany since the end of WWII. Include information on how East Germany came to be divided from West Germany, what life was like for people on each side, the kind of tensions between the two, and what brought about their reunification.

- Study the life of Brother Andrew, and write a short biographical sketch of him. Show his area of ministry, the obstacles he faced, God's miraculous provision and protection, and how the Church behind the Iron Curtain was strengthened.

- Read about the Korean War. Make a chart or diagram showing the major phases of this war. Be sure to include comments concerning the ongoing tension between North Korea and South Korea.

- Research and report on the United Nations. Show when and why it was formed, how it works, and how member nations are able to influence and affect situations in the world.

- Research and report on the Communist Revolution in China. Include the struggle between the Nationalist Party under Chiang Kai-Shek and the Communist Party under Mao Zedong, the Long March, and the results of the revolution.

- Research and report on the field of missionary aviation. Missionaries around the world often depend on the ministry of these "jungle pilots," and their service is many times both dangerous and exciting.

- Research and report on the Waorani people (known as "Auca" by their enemies), and how the Gospel has transformed their culture. Be sure to include the martyrdom of the five missionaries who first made contact with them, the work of Rachel Saint and Elisabeth Elliot, and the continuing work in the jungles of Ecuador.

- After WWII, there were indigenous people on Pacific islands who formed "cargo cults." They had seen the American Red Cross bring ship loads of supplies for the soldiers fighting in WWII without understanding where it was coming from or why it suddenly disappeared at the end of the war. On the island of Tanna, the "John Frum" people worshipped a red cross and waited for the coming of John Frum to tell them what to do. Read about these people in **National Geographic Magazine**, 1972, as well as the book, **The Man With the Bird on His Head**, by John Rush, and write a paper on how God moved mightily within this cargo cult.

- Read **Eternity in Their Hearts** by Don Richardson. Make a chart showing the redemptive analogies that missionaries were able to use to share the Gospel within each of these cultures. Every time you read about another redemptive analogy (such as in the question listed above), be sure to write it down on your chart. This is a lifetime study!

Brain Stretchers

- The issue of displaced Palestinian Arabs who have had no homeland since 1948 is complex and sobering. Research and report on why these people have not been accepted into other Arab lands (except in refugee camps) and why they have no home in Israel. Show the effects of living permanently in refugee camps, what political solutions have been tried, and whether there has been any success in these attempts.

- Investigate the involvement of the U.N. in troubled areas around the world. Include what they did and did not do in Korea, Hungary, Suez Canal, Palestine, the Cuban Missile Crisis, Viet Nam, through the struggles in Yugoslavia, and up to the present.

- Compare and contrast Taiwan with the People's Republic of China (Communist China). Show what life is like for the citizens of each country, their freedoms, restrictions, income, religion, etc.

- Study and write about the history of any one of the African countries since its European colonization. Be sure to include information on what the European country did to improve and to exploit its colony, how the colony received its independence, and what has happened since independence. Remember that in Africa, the geographical boundaries of most of the countries were drawn without regard to historical tribal boundaries. This has caused deep and unresolved conflicts between hostile people groups.

Vocabulary

decolonization	airlift	smuggler	persecution
emerging	partition	corruption	insurrection
martyrdom	homeland	Cold War	redemptive analogy
extermination	forum	Iron Curtain	limited war

In this unit there is a great emphasis on missionary and post-WWII terminology.

- Your assignment is to collect as many terms that apply to missionaries, African decolonization, or the Cold War, etc., that you find in this unit's study, and define them.

Hands On!

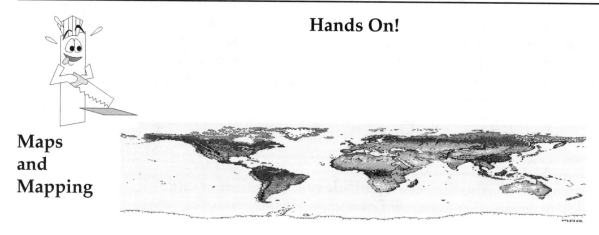

Maps and Mapping

- Using an atlas, encyclopedia, or other resource locate Palestine, Israel, the surrounding Arab countries, Korea, Taiwan, Ethiopia, Ghana, Ecuador, Tanna (in the South Pacific), Irian Jaya. What is the capital city, religion, population, major export, and type of government in each modern country? What is the status of Christianity in these countries?

- On a clean worksheet map, draw marks tracing the events of the wars against the new nation of Israel (beginning in 1948). Show where the invading armies came from, and how the borders of Israel changed with these wars.

- On a world map, draw lines tracing the events of the Korean War and of the Communist Revolution in China.

- Consult a relief map to discover the terrain found in Israel and Korea. Are there deserts, forest, mountains, islands? Label them. What kind of climate is typical in each of the different terrains? How did these different terrains and climates affect the wars which were fought, or the developing economic conditions, in these countries?

- On a world map, draw lines tracing missions activities. Connect each missionary's homeland to his place of ministry. Indicate sites of Bible translation. Indicate regions where the Gospel has been received and regions where it is still forbidden. Consider the terrain and climate in these countries and the affect they have on missions activity. Finally, notice which regions have no missions outreach. Pray for them.

The Mona Dot

Art Appreciation

*The artistic style known as "surrealism" began during the 1920's in France, but found wide public acceptance after WWII. This art style is intended to present the artist's understanding of reality - which was absurdity, fear, agony and despair. There is no hope in surrealism, and no possibility of escape. H. Rookmaaker, in **Modern Art and the Death of a Culture**, writes, "Yet surrealism is much more than a new style. Surrealism is no easy formula, not even a well-defined theory, and in the final analysis not even an artistic movement; it is a way of life and a direction of one's activity, an attitude of intellectual agony. Surrealism is revolutionary and destructive: the whole of western culture and its society are thrown away in a battle against all that exists..."*

- Look in the encyclopedia under the article, "Painting," to see an example of surrealistic art. Salvador Dali is perhaps the most famous of these painters. How would you describe this style of art? Do you think it accurately depicts the worldview of the artists? Why or why not? How would you share the Gospel with someone whose worldview was surrealistic?

*After the war, a new group of artists began creating a style of art known as abstract expressionism. The best known of these artists was Jackson Pollock, who simply spattered paint on a canvas and called it art. Alan Bowness, in **Modern European Art**, states, "Pollock defined the subject of his work as the act of painting itself: in pictures like "Number One" (1948) the paint tracks that the artist spattered across the canvas can theoretically be followed, and the experience of making it thus shared. That the result is more than beautiful decoration is due to the nervous intensity of the painter's line and his sensitive manipulation of pictorial space."*

- Look in the encyclopedia for the article on "Painting" to see Pollock's spatter painting. Would you agree with the statement made by Alan Bowness quoted above? Do you consider this more than "beautiful decoration"? Why or why not? Do you consider this less than "beautiful decoration"? Why or why not? How would you describe this painting? How does it differ from the art of the 1800's? How does it differ from cubism or surrealism?

Arts in Action

- Let's create some spatter art (just for the fun of it), and then discuss whether it truly is "art." Outside, set up poster board, butcher paper, an old sheet - whatever you would like to spatter. With tempera paint, house paint, or other liquid paints, try splattering your canvas "artistically." You may want to use only primary colors, or you may want to use lots of different colors. Consider which aspects are under your control (color, equipment, distance) and which aspects are not (gravity, design, overlap). When you are finished, give your work a title, let it dry completely, then set it up in the house and ask these questions:

#1) What is art? Define the term.
#2) What is Christian art? Define the term.
#3) Does this spatter painting qualify as either art or Christian art? Why or why not?
#4) Does this spatter painting reflect a certain worldview? Which one?

"... OOPS!! ..."

Architecture

The style of architecture popular immediately after WWII was known as the "international style." Because of the devastation caused by WWII, the reconstruction of Europe gave the architects of this style many opportunities to work on projects on an extensive scale. The international style can be characterized by geometric shapes, sometimes white walls, and a flat roof. The use of reinforced concrete (concrete with steel rods in it to strengthen the structure) enabled the architects to create large structures with lots of windows.

One of the most important architects of this style was Le Courbusier. His "Unités d'Habitation" were apartment buildings for 2,000 people concentrated in one tower block surrounded by parks. The advertising slogan for this was,"a revolutionary event, sun, space and greenery. If you want to raise a family in privacy, in silence and in natural surroundings..."

- Look for a picture of one of Le Courbusier's "Unités d'Habitation." One idea is to look in the encyclopedia under "France" for a representation of the architectural styles. Does this look like a place you could live "in natural surroundings"?

- Also, look for a picture of the luxury apartments built by Mies van der Rohe in Chicago around Lake Michigan, or the Seagram Building in New York City which he designed. How would you describe this architecture?

Science

After WWII, there was a tremendous amount of inventing going on. Some of it was "high-tech," but many things were invented to be labor-saving, time-saving, and food-saving devices for the average person. Here are some examples:

- George de Mestral stole an idea from the cockleburs in his socks and his dog's coat and invented the fastener Velcro in 1948.
- Pillsbury & General Mills began marketing prepared cake mixes in 1949.
- George Stephen invented an all-metal enclosed grill - the Weber grill - 1950.
- Marion Donovan developed disposable diapers from shower curtain and absorbent padding in 1951.
- Bette Nesmith, a Texas secretary, invented Liquid Paper® in 1954 to cover up mistakes made while typing.
- Frozen TV dinners were introduced in the U.S. in 1954.

- Create your own labor-saving, time-saving, or food-saving invention. You may want to keep your eyes and ears open to find out what people need and wish someone would invent! Your invention might be very simple or it might be very complex. I would love to hear what you come up with!

Music

Francis Poulenc (1899-1963) was a French composer who is considered to be one of the major liturgical composers of the twentieth century. The story of how Poulenc, who was known to his friends as a light-hearted, witty, frivolous man, came to be writing such powerful religious music in the latter part of his life is fascinating. In 1936, a close friend was killed in an automobile accident. Poulenc later said, "The horrible snuffing-out of this musician so full of vitality had absolutely stupefied me. Ruminating on the frailty of our human condition, I was once again attracted to the spiritual life... You now know the true source of inspiration for my religious works."

*Poulenc's music, rich and original, was based on the great masters of the past - Bach, Mozart, Chopin, Tchaikovsky, Puccini, Debussy, and others. Jane Stuart Smith, in **The Gift of Music**, writes: "It was not that he had no ideas himself, but because of his love for the music of these composers he made their music become a part of him. The music of Poulenc is as personal as any composed in this century."*

• Listen to Poulenc's "Mass in G Major" or "Gloria." The "Mass in G Major" is reserved and calm, while the "Gloria" is a work of joy and happiness in God. How would you compare this music to the music of other composers? How does it compare to the music sung in your church?

Cooking

In studying about Korea in this unit, we have the opportunity to sample some of its wonderful food!

Barbecued Short Ribs

3 pounds beef short ribs, trimmed of fat & gristle
Marinade:
2 Tbsp. fresh ginger root, peeled and minced   2 cloves garlic, crushed
1/2 cup soy sauce   1/4 cup tahini (sesame seed paste)
1/4 cup sugar   6 green onions, chopped

Combine marinade ingredients in a gallon zip-lock bag. Add ribs to marinade, locking the bag. Turn to distribute marinade evenly. Let stand 2 - 4 hours in the refrigerator, turning bag occasionally.

Preheat oven to 375 degrees, or fire up the charcoal grill. Place ribs on a roasting rack or on the grill. Reserve marinade. Roast ribs for 40 minutes, turning meat often and basting with the marinade. If cooking in the oven, raise oven heat to 450 degrees and continue cooking until they are crisp, about 5 minutes. Serves 4 to 6.

Idea Time

Creative Writing

- The vote at the U.N. has just been taken, and it's now official - Israel will become a nation! Your assignment is to interview people on the street in Jerusalem, both Jews and Arabs, to get their reaction to this momentous news. Help the folks back home to understand the various view points of the people here. Be sure to tell them your own impressions of Israel's chances against the Arab nations.

- Write a children's story about Brother Andrew - God's Smuggler. Tell in simple terms some of his adventures, and how God opened doors for him to bring Bibles into closed countries. You may want to contact Open Doors for more information on Brother Andrew's current activities.

- Ask neighbors or church friends for someone who fought in the Korean War. Then interview that person. Ask them about their experiences, what they learned, how it changed their lives. Write up the interview and submit it to your local newspaper, homeschool support group newsletter, or homeschooling magazine.

- Finish this poem about the decolonization of Africa:

Oh, how the mighty have fallen,
The empires who came now are gone...

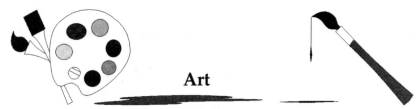

Art

- Draw a political cartoon of the way the Soviets were outmaneuvered by the Allies in the Berlin Airlift.

Drama

- Show the conflict between the Nationalists and Communists in China, including the Long March. You may want to try using mime for dramatic effect!

The Big Picture

- Though the world has changed drastically since the end of World War II, some things remain timeless. Jim Elliot's words, "A man is no fool to give up what he cannot keep to gain what he cannot lose," still speak wisdom. Share with family, friends and neighbors what you have learned in this unit about the importance of sacrifice and obedience in the Kingdom of God.

Resource List

Most of the books listed in this study guide are available from the library or interlibrary loan. However, the Christian titles and a few of the other wonderful resources listed will have to be purchased from homeschool providers, Christian bookstores, etc. The following is a list of some of the homeschool providers we know carry these materials. Call for their catalogs.

There are many other booksellers out there who may also be able to help you.

Farm Country General Store
1-800-551-3276

Christian Book Distributors
1-978-977-5000

Sing & Learn
1-972-278-1973

Lifetime Books and Gifts
1-800-377-0390

The Book Peddler
1-800-928-1760

Home Learning Center
1-406-257-5440

God's World Book Club
1-800-951-2665

Rainbow Resources
1-309-937-3385

Diana Waring - History Alive!
1-605-642-7583

Children's Books
1-800-344-3198

Builder Books
1-509-826-6021

In His Steps
1-800-583-1336

YWAM Publishing
1-800-922-2143

Sycamore Tree
1-800-779-6750

Education Express
(360) 452-3925

Cornerstone Curriculum Project
1-972-235-5149

Geography Matters
1-800-426-4650

Ferg 'N Us
1-610-282-0401

Adventure Safari
(612) 757-8107

Cadron Creek Christian Curriculum
(505) 534-1496

And for our international friends:

Christian Education Services
New Zealand
Fax: 011-64-9-410-3933

Canadian Home Education Resources
Calgary, Canada
(403) 253-9727

Maple Ridge Books
Ontario, Canada
(519) 986-2684

Diana Waring - History Alive!
Order form to copy and share with your friends.
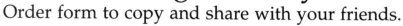

Name:_____

Address:_____

City:_____

State:_____ **Zip:**_____ **Phone:** (_____)_____

e-mail:_____

(You may order by telephone, fax, or by mailing us this order form.)

Contact us:
Diana Waring - History Alive!
P.O. Box 378
Spearfish, SD 57783
fax/phone: (605) 642-7583
www.dianawaring.com
e-mail: *diana@dianawaring.com*

	Price:	Qty:	Total:
Homeschool Books:			
Beyond Survival: A Guide to Abundant-life Homeschooling	$12.99		
Things We Wish We'd Known	$12.99		
Digging Deeper Study Guides:			
Ancient Civilizations & The Bible: Book A - Creation to Christ	$19.95		
Ancient Civilizations & The Bible Elementary Activity Guide	$11.95		
Romans, Reformers, Revolutionaries: Book B - Resurrection to the French Revolution	$22.95		
All Glory, Laud, and Honor: Seventeen Centuries of Christian Hymns (cassette)	$9.95		
All Glory, Laud, and Honor: Seventeen Centuries of Christian Hymns (CD)	$15.95		
World Empires, World Missions, World Wars: Book C - Napoleon to WWII	$22.95		
Maps/Timeline Packs:			
Maps/Timeline Pack - AC (to accompany Digging Deeper Study Guide, Book A)	$19.95		
Maps/Timeline Pack - RRR (to accompany Digging Deeper Study Guide, Book B)	$19.95		
Maps/Timeline Pack - WWW (to accompany Digging Deeper Study Guide, Book C)	$19.95		
History Seminars on Audio Cassette:			
What in the World's Going On Here? - Volume 1: Creation to the French Revolution	$20.95		
What in the World's Going On Here? - Volume 2: Napoleon to World War II	$20.95		
True Tales from the Times of: Ancient Civilizations & The Bible	$8.95		
True Tales from the Times of: Romans, Reformers, Revolutionaries	$8.95		
True Tales from the Times of: World Empires, World Missions, World Wars	$8.95		
History Via the Scenic Route: 4 1/2 hour audio-tape workshop	$20.95		
Homeschool Seminars on Audio Cassette:			
Beyond Survival: 90 minute audio-tape workshop	$8.95		
The Hilarious Homeschool: 90 minute audio-tape workshop	$8.95		
Heroes of the Faith: 90 minute audio-tape workshop	$8.95		
History Alive! - Through Music:			
America: 1750-1890	$19.99		
Westward Ho!: The Heart of the Old West	$19.99		
Musical Memories of Laura Ingalls Wilder	$19.99		
Homeschool Seminars on Video Cassette:			
Beyond Survival Homeschooling Class on Video	$59.95		
Package Deals:			
Package Deal #1: Ancient Civilizations & The Bible	$58.75		
Package Deal #2: Romans, Reformers, Revolutionaries	$61.75		
Package Deal #3: World Empires, World Missions, World Wars	$61.75		
Package Deal #4: Deluxe package including both #1 and #2	$109.75		
Package Deal #5: Deluxe package including #1, #2, and #3	$170.75		

Please make checks payable to:	**Subtotal:**
Diana Waring - History Alive!	**Add 10% Shipping (min. $3):**
P.O. Box 378, Spearfish, SD 57783	**SD residents add 4% sales tax:**
Visa/Mastercard accepted	**Total:**

Diana Waring - History Alive!
Order form to copy and share with your friends.

Name:_____

Address:_____

City:_____

State:_____ Zip:_____ Phone: (_____)_____

e-mail:_____

Contact us:
Diana Waring - History Alive!
P.O. Box 378
Spearfish, SD 57783
fax/phone: (605) 642-7583
www.dianawaring.com
e-mail: *diana@dianawaring.com*

You may order by telephone, fax, or by mailing us this order form.

	Price:	Qty:	Total:
Homeschool Books:			
Beyond Survival: A Guide to Abundant-life Homeschooling	$12.99		
Things We Wish We'd Known	$12.99		
Digging Deeper Study Guides:			
Ancient Civilizations & The Bible: Book A - Creation to Christ	$19.95		
Ancient Civilizations & The Bible Elementary Activity Guide	$11.95		
Romans, Reformers, Revolutionaries: Book B - Resurrection to the French Revolution	$22.95		
All Glory, Laud, and Honor: Seventeen Centuries of Christian Hymns (cassette)	$9.95		
All Glory, Laud, and Honor: Seventeen Centuries of Christian Hymns (CD)	$15.95		
World Empires, World Missions, World Wars: Book C - Napoleon to WWII	$22.95		
Maps/Timeline Packs:			
Maps/Timeline Pack - AC (to accompany Digging Deeper Study Guide, Book A)	$19.95		
Maps/Timeline Pack - RRR (to accompany Digging Deeper Study Guide, Book B)	$19.95		
Maps/Timeline Pack - WWW (to accompany Digging Deeper Study Guide, Book C)	$19.95		
History Seminars on Audio Cassette:			
What in the World's Going On Here? - Volume 1: Creation to the French Revolution	$20.95		
What in the World's Going On Here? - Volume 2: Napoleon to World War II	$20.95		
True Tales from the Times of: Ancient Civilizations & The Bible	$8.95		
True Tales from the Times of: Romans, Reformers, Revolutionaries	$8.95		
True Tales from the Times of: World Empires, World Missions, World Wars	$8.95		
History Via the Scenic Route: 4 1/2 hour audio-tape workshop	$20.95		
Homeschool Seminars on Audio Cassette:			
Beyond Survival: 90 minute audio-tape workshop	$8.95		
The Hilarious Homeschool: 90 minute audio-tape workshop	$8.95		
Heroes of the Faith: 90 minute audio-tape workshop	$8.95		
History Alive! - Through Music:			
America: 1750-1890	$19.99		
Westward Ho!: The Heart of the Old West	$19.99		
Musical Memories of Laura Ingalls Wilder	$19.99		
Homeschool Seminars on Video Cassette:			
Beyond Survival Homeschooling Class on Video	$59.95		
Package Deals:			
Package Deal #1: Ancient Civilizations & The Bible	$58.75		
Package Deal #2: Romans, Reformers, Revolutionaries	$61.75		
Package Deal #3: World Empires, World Missions, World Wars	$61.75		
Package Deal #4: Deluxe package including both #1 and #2	$109.75		
Package Deal #5: Deluxe package including #1, #2, and #3	$170.75		

Please make checks payable to:
Diana Waring - History Alive!
P.O. Box 378, Spearfish, SD 57783
Visa/Mastercard accepted

Subtotal:	
Add 10% Shipping (min. $3):	
SD residents add 4% sales tax:	
Total:	